TIMES SQUARE ■ CHURCH

Presented to

From

Date

TIM DILENA

ETERNAL
GOLD

30 DAILY MESSAGES TO HELP YOU PERSEVERE
IN YOUR PURSUIT OF VICTORY

Printed in Canada

Published by Carpenter's Son Publishing, Franklin, TN.

ISBN: 978-1-956370-61-4

Cover Design by Hybrid Studios

Interior Design by Hybrid Studios

To the athletes who have given body, soul, and mind to be the best in your field: It's our honor to care for your spirit for the next 30 days.

"All good athletes train hard.
They do it for a gold medal that tarnishes and fades.
You're after one that's gold eternally."
—1 Corinthians 9:25, MSG

CONGRATULATIONS ON YOUR JOURNEY TO ETERNAL GOLD

I love the word convergence. At its simplest definition, it is when everything comes together. It is when the intense training, dieting, education, mentoring, and timing all come together. The goal is clear; the goal is simple. It's what every athlete hopes and prays their converging moment will result in the prize! The challenge, however, for the Christian athlete goes far beyond the prize. Their ultimate recognition is not where they hear the national anthem but where they hear the voice of the Father say, "Well done, good and faithful servant" (Matthew 25:21, NIV). They understand the reality of their present race, event, match, or game—while at the same time, never losing sight of the greater race. The greater race does not converge around five circles but a crown of thorns. It is a race that started the day we were born. The victory was determined the day Jesus died and rose again. The finish line is crossed in heaven when we see Jesus face-to-face.

We lay hold of the apostle Paul's words in 1 Corinthians 9:25 (MSG) when he says, "All good athletes train hard. They do it for a gold medal that tarnishes and fades. You're after one that's gold eternally." When all is said and done, I don't think anything will be sweeter than getting eternal gold in heaven.

The one person who best exemplified achieving the prize, and eternal gold in heaven, was Olympic gold medalist, Eric Liddell. One hundred years ago, Liddell competed in the 1924 Paris Olympics. Liddell lived with both goals in mind:

He said, "I believe God made me for a purpose. He made me for China [as a missionary], but He also made me fast. And when I run, I feel His pleasure."[1]

His story became the 1981 Academy Award-winning motion picture, Chariots of Fire. The movie describes the moment in the Olympics when Liddell refused to run in the 100-meter final because the race was on "the Lord's Day." A fellow British teammate relinquished his spot in the 400-meter final, which was scheduled for a Monday, to allow Liddell to run, even though he had not trained for that race. Nevertheless, Liddell ran the 400-meter, broke a world record, and won the gold! He won two gold medals that day. Eric Liddell received the smile of Scotland and the smile of heaven. The smile of heaven is eternal gold.

The apostle Peter sums it all up in his first epistle. Let his words sink into your soul:

> "What a God we have! And how fortunate we are to have him, this Father of our Master Jesus! Because Jesus was raised from the dead, we've been given a brand-new life and have everything to live for, including a future in heaven—and the future starts now! God is keeping careful watch over us and the future. The Day is coming when you'll have it all—life healed and whole. "I know how great this makes you feel, even though you have to put up with every kind of aggravation in the meantime. Pure gold put in the fire comes out of it proved pure; genuine faith put through this suffering comes out proved genuine. When Jesus wraps this all up, it's your faith, not your gold, that God will have on display as evidence of his victory" (1 Peter 1:3–7, MSG).

The ultimate victory is eternal gold!

---

1 Benge, J., & Benge, G. (1998). Eric Liddell: Something Greater Than Gold. Christian Heroes: Then & Now

LET'S SLAP
THE FLOOR
TODAY

Before there was Federer, Djokovic, and Nadal, there was the iconic American tennis player, Pete Sampras. When Sampras seemed to be at the peak of his career, he made a shocking move and decided to retire.

Sampras had a particular habit that he would do before every tennis match. In the locker room or wherever he was getting dressed, he would lace up his tennis shoes, and then he would take both hands and slap the floor.

That was his way of saying, "Okay, it's time!"

He said, "I always told myself, 'If you quit slapping, it's time to retire.'"

Sampras later recounted that after a few matches, he realized he wasn't slapping the floor like he used to. And that's when he retired.[2]

What is it that makes a person slap the floor? I have been pastoring for over 40 years, and I still slap the floor each day I get to go to work. I get pumped and genuinely excited to counsel, mentor, preach, write, and envision the future. How do we keep slapping the floor each day we wake up and not end up retiring early?

David, the psalmist, gives us a good reason for floor slapping in the book of Psalms: "This is the day which the Lord has made; let us rejoice and be glad in it" (Psalms 118:24, NASB).

There will be times you and I will not be excited about a certain meeting, a certain workout, a certain relationship we have to face—but what we can slap the floor about is the fact that this is God's day. Today is God's day, created by Him and given to us. Today is a gift.

American cartoonist Bil Keane once said it this way: "Yesterday's the past, tomorrow's the future, but today is a gift. That's why it's called the present."[3]

That is profound. Let's treat today as a gift from God. Let's get up and thank God that we are breathing and get to make the most of this day.

Today you get to compete. Today you get to do what you have been training all your life to do. Today you get to do it with the best in the world. Today you get to celebrate with some of the most important people in your life on the biggest stage. See today as a gift from God. Choose to rejoice in this day and slap the floor!

MY PRAYER TODAY

Dear Lord, I cannot change the past. I do not know what will happen tomorrow. But one thing I know for sure: You gave me a gift, and it is this day. I will do what the apostle Paul says and "make the best use of the time" (Ephesians 5:16, ESV). I will waste no days, knowing that time is precious. Today I thank You for Your gift of a new day—and I celebrate with the first of many floor slaps!

2 Reilly, R. (2003, June 16.) "Game, Set, Career." Sports Illustrated. Retrieved from https://vault.si.com/vault/2003/06/16/game-set-career

3 Dultz, T. (n.d.). "Who Said 'Yesterday Is History Tomorrow Is a Mystery Today Is a Gift'?" Retrieved from http://yesterdaytomorrowtodaypresent.blogspot.com/2015/08/yesterday-tomorrow-and-today-phrase.html

LET'S DIG IN THE RIGHT PLACE

In November 1975, a group of 75 incarcerated men started digging a secret tunnel designed to bring them to the other side of the wall of Saltillo Prison in northern Mexico. On April 18, 1976, they finally achieved their goal. However, they ended up tunneling into the nearby courtroom in which many of them had been sentenced. Court happened to be in session when they surfaced from their tunnel. The surprised judge immediately returned all 75 men to prison.[4]

Imagine doing all that work only to be sent right back to prison. This serves as a lesson for all of us—it is critical to know where we are going and to make sure we are digging in the right place!

In order to grow big, we must dig deep. Whenever you see someone growing in an area or skill, remember that depth must accompany growth. I live in New York City, and when they build the city's skyscrapers, they must first dig down deep. The depth determines the height. This holds true not only for skyscrapers but also for building our lives, our skills, and our future.

We are told in the Gospel of Luke that Jesus experienced growth in four areas when emerging from childhood to manhood: "And Jesus grew in wisdom and stature, and in favor with God and man" (Luke 2:52, NIV).

There is no growth unless there is depth, and no one will ever be deeper than Jesus. That means if Jesus grew in these four areas, we should grow in them, too. Jesus grew mentally, physically, spiritually, and relationally. He kept His growth in balance. I have seen people grow physically in their sport but fail with God and with people. I have also watched people grow in wisdom and education but die early because they did not give attention to their physical bodies. Jesus' life exemplifies balance. Jesus showed us where to dig and go deep.

The area that often gets overlooked for those who are growing physically—and even for those growing in understanding and wisdom—is the spiritual side. Lopsided foundations will eventually cause things to topple over when the storms come. Let's dig in the right place. Let's dig where Jesus dug. Let's grow proportionately.

One day my body will fail; one day my mind will not be as sharp. One day I will be forgotten by the people who now surround me. But the one growth spot that will have eternal ramifications and an eternal payoff is the spiritual side. Let's go deeper with God, for that growth never stops!

MY PRAYER TODAY

Jesus, help me to grow like You grew. I need wisdom today in all the decisions I must make. I am asking You to watch over me physically. I desire healthy relationships with the people around me. And most importantly, I want to have a healthy relationship with You. I know my relationship with You grows with daily obedience. I ask You to teach me to be sensitive to Your voice and to obey with joy!

4 Campus Life, September, 1980

THEY CALL THEM LITTLE FOXES, AND THEY CAN MESS UP EVERYTHING

On a cold January morning, I remember being in my junior year in college in a corporate finance class when we were told that there had just been a national tragedy. The Challenger Space Shuttle exploded shortly after liftoff, killing all seven astronauts.

In hindsight, we know that the Challenger deaths could have been avoided. On that fateful winter morning of January 28, 1986, the Space Shuttle Challenger stood poised for launch. Overnight, temperatures had plummeted into the 20s. At liftoff, it was a crisp 36 degrees Fahrenheit. Four-foot icicles still clung ominously to the launch tower. One of the engineers was concerned that because of those temperatures, the O-rings sealing the sections of each booster might be more likely to leak. The rings had never been tested below 51 degrees Fahrenheit. Nevertheless, the launch went ahead as scheduled. Seventy-three seconds later, six brave astronauts and one enthusiastic schoolteacher lost their lives when the O-rings failed.[5]

We see how something so small could cause such a horrific disaster. The O-ring was a little fox.

Solomon is considered to be the richest man who ever lived. Jeff Bezos, Bill Gates, Elon Musk, Warren Buffett, and Mark Zuckerberg are not even in the ballpark of Solomon's riches. This man gave us a gift when he gave us the books of Proverbs, Ecclesiastes, and Song of Solomon. They contain Solomon's advice to humanity. One of his pieces of advice is to keep an eye on little things that spoil big things, which he describes as little foxes.

These are his words: "Catch the foxes for us, the little foxes that spoil the vineyards, for our vineyards are in blossom" (Song of Solomon 2:15, ESV).

Solomon was warning us that little things can mess up everything. In fact, he tells us that such foxes seem to come at the worst time. They show up hours before launch time or right as things are in bloom. When we are about to see the fruit of all we worked hard for—what may have taken months or years of preparation—is precisely when sabotage shows up. When you work hard as an athlete, astronaut, architect, or gardener, you don't want to see things suddenly jeopardized by something so little. It came for Solomon's vineyard right when things were about to bloom.

Keep an eye out for little things that can upset everything.

Keep an eye on little things that show up just before the event, the launch, or the harvest. Little things can be an argument, a person you have not seen for a long time, or a memory of a past failure. It could even be as minute as not hearing your alarm and waking up late. It's a little fox that spoils the vine.

You don't have to go fox hunting every day, but you do have to be able to identify a fox. It is realizing that this is a little thing, and it is trying to get into your vineyard. That's when you need to be fast and thorough. Stop the fox by apologizing to your spouse, ignoring a negative social media post by someone you don't even know, or realizing that you can't change what just happened and need to move forward. Foxes will distract, demand time, and give nothing back but destruction. You have dug, weeded, planted, and protected. Now that it's time for blossoms, remember that it's also time for little foxes. Do not let a little thing mess up the big thing that is ahead of you today.

Lord, thank You for giving me the ability to see gifts and talents in my life blossom. I know that when You want to use me most, the devil will come with his best. I can identify the big stuff, but I need Your help today to see the little foxes. By Your grace, I will blossom for Your glory, and I will kill some little foxes today, too!

MY PRAYER TODAY

5 King, P. H. (2019, March 12). "Shuttle Launch Was Warned About Cold: Engineers Suggested No Liftoff Below 51." Los Angeles Times. Retrieved from https://www.latimes.com/archives/la-xpm-1986-02-12-mn-27458-story.html

04

HE JUST
SHOWED
UP

One of the longest standing ovations in sports history was not for someone who hit the most home runs, sunk the most three pointers, ran the fastest race, or scored the most touchdowns. That standing ovation was for someone who showed up for work every day. In fact, he showed up for 2,131 consecutive games. He never missed a day of work as a baseball player. His name was Cal Ripken Jr. When he broke Lou Gehrig's record, the Baltimore crowd stood for 22 minutes to honor Ripken as he came to the plate.[6] With so many variables that can hinder you from showing up, Ripken pulled off a miracle.

Good stuff happens when you simply show up. That's what happened to a New Testament priest named Zechariah. The Gospel of Luke tells us that he showed up to work one day because his name was on the list to serve in the temple:

> "Once when Zechariah's division was on duty and he was serving as priest before God, he was chosen by lot, according to the custom of the priesthood, to go into the temple of the Lord and burn incense" (Luke 1:8–9, NIV).

On that day, not only did Zechariah show up, but an angel showed up, also!

> "Then an angel of the Lord appeared to him, standing at the right side of the altar of incense. When Zechariah saw him, he was startled and was gripped with fear. But the angel said to him: 'Do not be afraid, Zechariah; your prayer has been heard. Your wife Elizabeth will bear you a son, and you are to call him John'" (Luke 1:11–13, NIV).

A longtime prayer for a child was going to be answered, and the answer would come through an angel while Zechariah was doing his regular work shift. If ever there were a story to encourage us to show up for work, it is Zechariah's story! All of heaven was poised to send the archangel, Gabriel, to deliver the good news. One can only speculate what would have happened had Zechariah called in sick that day. Thankfully, he showed up, and he left work that day with more than a paycheck—he received an answer to prayer! He and Elizabeth were going to have a son.

Angel visits can potentially happen to any of us at any time. As you prepare for your day, be all there. The great Christian missionary, Jim Elliot, said it like this: "Wherever you are, be all there! Live to the hilt every situation you believe to be the will of God."[7] As you get ready for today, be all there and be all in, for who knows if an angel will show up!

Lord, Your Word says: "This is the day that the Lord has made; we will rejoice and be glad in it" (Psalms 118:24). You gave me today as a gift. Let me not waste it halfheartedly. Let all of me show up for all of Your day that You have made. The first thing I will do today is attack it with joy and gladness!

MY PRAYER TODAY

6 "Cal Ripken Jr. Streak Oral History." (n.d.). MLB.Com. Retrieved from https://www.mlb.com/rangers/news/featured/cal-ripken-jr-streak-oral-history

7 "Stillness—Elisabeth Elliot." (n.d.). Elisabeth Elliot. Retrieved from https://elisabethelliot.org/resource-library/devotionals/stillness-3/

05

I NEED
TO FIND
MY 26 FEET

I never thought I would experience an earthquake in New York City, but I did. I also never thought I would experience one of the worst hurricanes in American history in New York City, but I did. It was called Hurricane Sandy. The damage from Long Island to Manhattan and into New Jersey was devastating. Over the course of 48 hours, Hurricane Sandy wiped out the power for hundreds of thousands of New Yorkers, left many homeless, and caused an estimated $70 billion in damage, crippling the largest city in America.[8] It seemed no one was left unaffected in New York City ... except for one group.

I heard some years ago about what fish do during hurricanes and tropical storms. I recall being told that they descend 26 feet below sea level, which is where they are able to evade the turbulent waters. At that depth, they can find peace while those on the surface are dealing with mayhem.

If this is true, we all need to find our 26 feet. Each day, the surface of our lives can get crazy, so we must know how to take a deep dive. Some try to do it by blasting music on their Apple AirPods to drown out the noise. But I have discovered that even with the best headphones, our souls need to find their 26 feet every day.

I began to ask God to help me find my 26 feet, which brought me to the book of Psalms. The psalmist, David, was in a storm caused by people in his life. No one can say for sure who David had in mind when he penned Psalm 109. It could have been Saul who despised him, regarding him as a threat to his throne. Or perhaps it was his own son, Absalom, who rebelled and stole the kingdom from him. It might have been Doeg, who snitched on David's whereabouts so his killers could track him. Or maybe it was his trusted counselor, Ahithophel, who betrayed him out of bitterness. We don't know the who of Psalm 109, but we do know that we all have had a who in our life that caused a storm for us—someone who betrayed us, lied about us, hated us, broke our confidence, or wreaked havoc for us through their words—be it from their mouth or their keyboard. Look at what David wrote:

> "God of my praise, do not be silent! For they have opened a wicked and deceitful mouth against me; they have spoken against me with a lying tongue. They have also surrounded me with words of hatred, and fought against me without cause. In return for my love they act as my accusers" (Psalms 109:1-4, NASB).

David's storm consisted of lies, deceit, and accusations. To add insult to injury, it was coming from people he called friends and had shown love to. Clearly, this was one of David's lowest moments.

Thankfully, it only took four verses to find 26 feet. It came in the form of five words, which we are going to borrow for our deep dives during the storms.

David concluded verse 4 by saying, " ... but I am in prayer."

Did you see the deep dive?

"But I am in prayer!"

Those five powerful words helped get David to calm water, and we can use them, as well. These five words are how we descend to 26 feet. So when you are hit with a crisis, an accusation, a family death, or when you get slandered or attacked, go deeper! Go to 26 feet.

Decide today that it will be said of you: "But I am in prayer."

Charles Stanley, the great Atlanta pastor, said it like this: "The shortest distance between our problems and their solutions is the distance between our knees and the floor."[9]

I have to tell you, there will be a lot of 26 feet deep dives throughout the day!

MY PRAYER TODAY

Lord, my prayer today is being prayed at 26 feet. There is so much happening on the surface that I need a quiet place. Today, I come to You because You have invited me to this depth. I believe Your words when You said in Matthew 11:28 (MSG), "Are you tired? Worn out? Burned out on religion? Come to me. Get away with me and you'll recover your life." There is recovery in Your presence. There is a place for me at 26 feet.

8 Rott, N. (2021, May 18). "Climate Change's Impact on Hurricane Sandy Has a Price: $8 Billion." NPR. Retrieved from https://www.npr.org/2021/05/18997666304/climate-changes-impact-on-hurricane-sandy-has-a-price-8-billion

9 Stanley, C. (2011). Handle With Prayer: Unwrap the Source of God's Strength for Living. David C Cook

WHAT'S ON THE INSIDE DETERMINES THE EFFECTS OF THE OUTSIDE

Let me ask you a simple question: Which is easier to crush, a Coke can that is full or empty? This is not a trick question. Obviously, the empty can is easier to crush. When it is sealed and full of Coke, it takes a lot more pressure to crush that can. The same could be said of us. What is in us determines the effects of what happens to us. Let's say it another way: Who is in us will determine how we are affected by what happens to us.

Before you become a Christian, you are empty inside. When you become born again, the void is filled with the Holy Spirit. Life may be tough on the outside, but the good news is that you have what it takes to face it because of Who is on the inside.

The apostle John said it like this: "Ye are of God, little children, and have overcome them: because greater is he that is in you, than he that is in the world" (1 John 4:4, KJV).

No matter what pressure you may face today, remember that Christ in you is what prevents the pressure from crushing you. The Coke can is your life; the contents is Jesus. He is enough to help you get through whatever this day may hold.

Some years ago, the U.S. Navy experienced one of its worst underwater disasters. The nuclear submarine Thresher descended too deep and was crushed by the ocean pressure. It sank to almost 8,000 feet, where remains of the steel submarine were found. The thick steel was unable to withstand the pressure of the water in their deep dive. Tragically, 129 lives were lost that day.

What is fascinating is how a little fish in the same depths can swim around without any worry of being crushed or imploding. These fish are not made of steel but are made by God. Why aren't they crushed? God created fish with an internal pressure system that perfectly corresponds to the pressure they face around them. In other words, they can happily swim at great depths because of what is on the inside of them.

The apostle Paul described Who is on the inside to help us with life's pressures that we constantly face on the outside.

> "But we have this treasure in jars of clay to show that this all-surpassing power is from God and not from us. We are hard pressed on every side, but not crushed; perplexed, but not in despair; persecuted, but not abandoned; struck down, but not destroyed" (2 Corinthians 4:7–9, NIV).

Hard pressed on every side but not crushed—all because we have this treasure, Jesus, in our lives.

MY PRAYER TODAY

Lord, I thank You that You are in my life. When I invited You to come in and change me, You came in and resided in me. Your presence in my life is my protection. May I be so filled with Jesus today, leaving no room for anything else. Help me to navigate through today's depths. Though the pressures of life may crush others, they won't crush me because You are in me. I realize today that if You are for me, who can be against me? (See Romans 8:31.)

---

10 Yancey, P., & Stafford, T. (1979). Secrets of the Christian Life. Zondervan Publishing Company

YOU GET TO PICK WHAT YOU THINK

In Philippians 4:8 (NKJV), Paul wrote, "Whatever things are true, whatever things are noble, whatever things are just, whatever things are pure, whatever things are lovely, whatever things are of good report, if there is any virtue and if there is anything praiseworthy—think on these things."

"Think on these things" is a command, not a suggestion. God would never command His people to do something that they couldn't do. That means you really can "think on these things." In other words, you get to pick what you think about.

Christian author, Max Lucado, explained it this way:

> "You probably know this, but in case you don't, I am so thrilled to give you the good news ... you can pick what you ponder. You didn't select your birthplace or birth date. You didn't choose your parents or siblings. There are many things in life over which you have no choice. But the greatest activity of life is well within your dominion. You can choose what you think about. You can be the air traffic controller of your mental airport. You occupy the control tower and can direct the mental traffic of your world. Thoughts circle above, coming and going. If one of them lands, it is because you gave it permission. If it leaves, it is because you directed it to do so."[11]

When we fail to control our thoughts, some call it "stinkin' thinking." Our thoughts even affect our immune system. Dr. Michael Jacobson cited a study in which patients were asked to recall various types of emotional experiences while doctors monitored how the thoughts affected their bodies. Each patient was asked to relive the experiences in their minds for five minutes. When the patients thought for five minutes about experiences that made them depressed, they found out that it affected the patients' immune system, and their antibody levels dropped 55%. Six hours later, their immune system was still depressed. But when the patients thought for five minutes about situations that made them happy, their antibody levels rose 40% and remained elevated six hours later. This is medical evidence that the thoughts we think affect our bodies, either positively or negatively.[12]

Thoughts can get stuck in us, but Paul says you can get them unstuck from your mind as you start thinking about the right things. The next verse is where Paul gives the best way for this to happen.

> "The things which you learned and received and heard and saw in me, these do, and the God of peace will be with you" (Philippians 4:9, NKJV).

Paul was essentially reminding us, "You are not an only child in the faith. You need to glean from the experience of other people. Walk with someone who has walked it out already."

If you battle anxiety, surround yourself with others who have learned how to trust the Lord when life is overwhelming. Spend time with people who understand the complexities of anxiety and the keys to success. Ask them questions. Ponder their answers. Study their lives. Listen to their stories. Learn from them, and put it into action.

Perhaps it is time to make an appointment with a doctor or wise counselor, ask a friend to meet you for coffee, join a small group at church, or simply read an encouraging book about someone—maybe even the apostle Paul—who learned how to hand their anxious cares over to the Lord. Let God's peace in their lives influence the anxiety in yours. We all need the right people in our lives. God never intended for you to walk alone.

When Jim Jones was five years old, he was shuttled from his family home in Mississippi to northern Michigan to live with his grandparents. The trauma of the move caused him to stutter. Hating school because other kids snickered when he spoke, he learned to speak as little as possible, consoling himself by writing poetry. When Jim was a teenager, a new teacher came to the school, Donald Crouch, a devout Mennonite and retired professor who loved poetry. Crouch discovered Jim also loved and wrote poetry. He urged the boy to read his poems aloud. Jim refused. But in class one morning, Crouch tricked him.

The boy had turned in a poem he had written, and Crouch said, "I don't think you wrote this."

When Jim, stuttering, insisted he had, Crouch forced him to prove it by reciting it from memory to the class. Nervously, while the other kids smirked and whispered, Jim began to recite his poem. He found, as many who stutter have discovered, that the rhythms of poetry enabled his words to flow naturally. That day, Jim did not stutter.

He continued to practice reading poetry and learned he had an excellent, resonant voice. After he graduated, he went on to earn his college degree, served in the army, and returned to study drama on the GI Bill. Today we know Jim as James Earl Jones, a superb actor famous for his acting talent and for his sonorous, inimitable voice. Who can forget him as Darth Vader's voice in the original Star Wars films? But again, that's not the end of the story.

Years later, at the pinnacle of his career, Jones was asked to record the New Testament. He remembered Donald Crouch—the man who had given him victory over his disability all those years ago—and dedicated the reading to him.

As Jones put it, Crouch "not only helped to guide me to the author of the Scriptures, but, as the father of my resurrected voice, also helped me find abundant life."[13]

When you introduce people to the author of the Scriptures, you resurrect within them things they never knew were there. It all starts by thinking about the things God wants you to think about and then helping others to do the same.

MY PRAYER TODAY

Lord, Your Word tells me to love You with all my soul and all my mind. You wouldn't ask me to do that if I were not able to. So today I am going to pick what I think about. The first thing I will start thinking about is the fact that You love me. I choose not to allow any thought to land in my mind that would contradict the greatest thought my mind could ever ponder. Amen.

11 Lucado, M. (2018, February 16). Tweet. Retrieved from https://twitter.com/MaxLucado/status/964507139820670976?lang=en

12 Jacobson, M. (1996, October). "Stress and the Heart."

13 Jones, J. E. (2022, June 28) "Guideposts Classics: James Earl Jones on the Importance of Mentoring." Guideposts. Retreived from https://guideposts.org/positive-living/health-and-wellness/life-advice/finding-life-purpose/guideposts-classics-james-earl-jones-on-the-importance-of-mentoring/

EXTRAORDINARY
PEOPLE
!!!

I want to teach you a new way to say the word extraordinary. When we break it up into two words, we see its true definition. Extraordinary is really just extra plus ordinary. Extraordinary is ordinary plus one more thing.

One of my friends was meeting with a former champion welterweight boxer. He told my friend that he used to get up every night at midnight and do 200 push-ups and 100 sit-ups. When my friend asked him why, he said he would tell himself that while his opponent was sleeping, he was doing something extra to get the edge on winning. He was pursuing extraordinary. One extra thing is often the only thing that stands between ordinary and extraordinary.

The word extraordinary was used in the Bible to describe only one person: Daniel. As a teenage boy, Daniel was taken as a prisoner of war when his nation was taken captive by Babylon. He was brought into the king's palace, and, on this foreign soil, we are told that he possessed an "extraordinary spirit." It distinguished Daniel from the other government workers in Persia. Here is what the Bible says:

> "It seemed good to Darius to appoint 120 satraps over the kingdom, that they would be in charge of the whole kingdom, and over them three commissioners (of whom Daniel was one), that these satraps might be accountable to them, and that the king might not suffer loss. Then Daniel began distinguishing himself among the commissioners and satraps because he possessed an

extraordinary spirit, and the king planned to appoint him over the entire kingdom" (Daniel 6:1-3, NASB).

An extraordinary spirit promoted a POW over the entire nation!

The best way to be extraordinary is to become a spiritual appraiser each day.

The apostle Paul says in 1 Corinthians 2:15 (NASB), "But he who is spiritual appraises all things."

The word appraise means to set a value on how much something is worth after thorough examination. An appraisal considers the question: Is it worth the cost it is demanding of me? We are told to do appraisals on all things. After closer examination, is it worth holding onto unforgiveness and bitterness? After closer examination, is it worth it to neglect reading my Bible for more time on social media? After closer examination, is it worth it to spend my money on more things? Extraordinary people are great at spiritually appraising all things. They constantly ask themselves, "Is it worth it?"

Oklahoma pastor, Craig Groeschel, said, "Successful people do consistently what normal people do occasionally."[14]

I believe extraordinary is available but rarely pursued.

My wife texted me this quote the other day: "Go the extra mile; it's never crowded."

I think the most extraordinary thing about Daniel's story are the dates. Daniel was a teenager when he was brought into captivity in 605 BC, the date of Daniel chapter 1. The verses we looked at in Daniel 6 took place in 539 BC. That was 66 years later! By that time, Daniel was around 80 years old and was still being called extraordinary by those around him! Extraordinary has no time limits. Go the extra mile. Do the extra thing. Distinguish yourself. Be extraordinary.

Lord, I want to be extraordinary. Show me how to appraise all things spiritually. May I be sharpened over the years to see and appraise things more accurately. Help me today to identify the extra thing I can add to this ordinary day to make it extraordinary.

MY PRAYER TODAY

14 Groeschel, C. (2015, November 15). Tweet. Retrieved from https://twitter.com/craiggroeschel/status/665938425099370497?lang=en

09

JUST
DELIVER
THE CHEESE

I want to tell you a cheese story. Many of us know the guy who delivered it. However, the cheese part of the story is easily missed as a 9-foot man tends to dominate the story. The cheese delivery man was David, and the giant in the story was, of course, Goliath. But how did David end up with that slingshot in a battle that kickstarted his destiny toward becoming the king of Israel?

It all started with delivering cheese to his brothers:

> "Then Jesse said to David his son, 'Take now for your brothers an ephah of this roasted grain and these ten loaves and run to the camp to your brothers. Bring also these ten cuts of cheese to the commander of their thousand, and look into the welfare of your brothers, and bring back news of them. For Saul and they and all the men of Israel are in the valley of Elah, fighting with the Philistines.'" (1 Samuel 17:17–20, NASB).

David was on orders from his father to bring food to his soldier brothers and to check on their well-being. Little did David know that simply obeying his father would change the trajectory of his life. David ended up meeting Goliath through cheese. What you consider to be a mundane task can actually be a door to your future!

If David had thought he was better than a cheese delivery man, he would have missed the door. I believe entry ramps into your destiny begin with humble little tasks that don't even match what you want to do. It is God's humility test.

A Chinese missionary from many years ago named Hudson Taylor, said, "A little thing is a little thing, but faithfulness in a little thing is a big thing."[15]

Don't dismiss little things, for they really may be big things. What you define as trivial can actually be massive!

A cheese delivery is doing something for others that may not get noticed or praised—but it can have monumental ramifications later down the road. Because David chose to do what seemed trivial, his brothers were able to enjoy a good meal on the battlefield. The commanders also got to eat from David's delivery. And an anxious father was able to receive news of his sons' welfare. Nowhere in this task can anyone see David's win—except God.

Here is what I have learned in my life: Don't try to find your destiny. Just say "yes" to small tasks, and your destiny will find you. David wasn't led straight to the battle that would forever be known as "David and Goliath." He was asked to do something small that eventually opened the door for something really big—something that would be known for ages to come. He wasn't even inspired to run the errand; he was simply doing what his dad had asked him to do.

What you see as a mundane cheese delivery is so much more in God's eyes. In David's case, God saw a way to get a young shepherd boy noticed—the last person anyone would have considered to fight the Philistine giant.

So don't ever say, "I don't do cheese."

Go from the beginning of the Bible to the end, and you will see over and over the story of men and women who had a servant's heart, mind, and spirit. And the world is a better place because:

Moses didn't say, "I don't do deserts."

Noah didn't say, "I don't do boats."

Jeremiah didn't say, "I don't do weeping."

Amos didn't say, "I don't do speeches."

Rahab didn't say, "I don't do hiding spies."

Ruth didn't say, "I don't do mothers-in-law."

Mary didn't say, "I don't do virgin births."

Mary Magdalene didn't say, "I don't do feet."

Paul didn't say, "I don't do letters."

Jesus didn't say, "I don't do crosses."

Let the words of the great evangelist, D. L. Moody, challenge you today: "There are many of us that are willing to do great things for the Lord, but few of us are willing to do little things ... for a great God."[16]

MY PRAYER TODAY

Thank You, Jesus, for being the perfect example of a servant. Your Word says in Philippians 2 that You came from heaven and became a servant. If You left heaven to go to a cross for us, then I can surely get up off this couch or out of this bed and do something for someone else today. And who knows? In the process of helping someone else, I may run into a surprise—my destiny. Make me a servant today, no matter how small the task.

15 Broomhall, A. J. (1984). Hudson Taylor & China's Open Century

16 Dwight L. Moody Quote. (n.d.). A-Z Quotes. Retrieved from https://www.azquotes.com/quote/203921

BE CAREFUL OF GETTING DOWN TO OTHER PEOPLE'S LEVEL WHEN YOU ARE DOING SOMETHING GREAT

You may know that John Grisham wrote all these books that went on to become movies: "The Firm," "A Time To Kill," "The Client," "The Chamber," "Runaway Jury," "The Pelican Brief," and "The Rainmaker." But what you may not know is how he became a best-selling author. Grisham was an attorney who wasn't satisfied with his job. He wanted to become a writer. He decided to start getting to work an hour or two earlier every day—the only quiet moments he could find—in order to write.

That was it! He got up earlier just to start writing before his workday began. Regardless of who laughed at him or assured him it was a waste of time, Grisham kept at it. He eventually went on to become one of the most prolific novelists of our time.[17]

In the Bible, a man named Nehemiah wasn't an attorney but a bartender for the king. He had a vision not to be a writer but a builder. His desire was to rebuild the wall of his beloved city, Jerusalem, to set them on the road to recovery after an invasion. It wasn't a few pages a day but a few bricks a day. Nearly 2,500 years ago, Nehemiah spearheaded the construction of a wall that would surround Jerusalem—parts of which still stand today! I have seen the ruins of that wall in Jerusalem, and it is a reminder that what God has asked you to do will outlive you.

During the rebuilding of the wall, Nehemiah was threatened, ridiculed, and had lies spread about him—all so that he would not accomplish his task. But the attack that was probably his greatest temptation came from people who just wanted to talk.

Be careful of stopping what God has called you to do in order to have conversations with people who are doing nothing with their lives. Nehemiah's response to these people on the ground level who wanted to talk is not only epic, it's worth borrowing for our own lives:

> "So I sent messengers to them, saying, "I am doing a great work and I cannot come down. Why should the work stop while I leave it and come down to you?" (Nehemiah 6:3, NASB).

"I am doing a great work and cannot come down" are words we all need to embrace. Someone said that there are two great days in our lives. The first is the day we were born. The second is when we discover why we were born. Nehemiah knew he was born to rebuild a wall for the future of the city he loved. When you know what God has called you to do, there will always be people on the ground level who want you to stop and talk to them. Those conversations will not push you forward. Those meetings will not make you better. Their words will not inspire you to be a greater wall builder. The bottom line is that they interrupt a great work for talking.

I'll never forget the words an old Methodist pastor once told me: "Whenever you say 'yes' to anything, there is 'less' of you for something else. Just make sure your 'yes' is worth the 'less.'"

Nehemiah knew his "yes" to their meeting was not worth the "less" of him for what God had called him to do!

MY PRAYER TODAY

Lord, there are many voices calling me off the wall every day. I need Your wisdom to know when to say "yes" as well as Your courage to say "no" to those who are distractions. Help me to see clearly when something is calling me away from the great work You have for me. I want to give you my best and nothing less!

---

17 Bill Moyers Journal, Archive. (n.d.). PBS. Retrieved from http://www.pbs.org/moyers/journal/archives/grishamexcl_flash.html.

I'M GIVING IT EVERYTHING I'VE GOT

Several years ago, right before the Super Bowl, I read an amazing article in The Wall Street Journal called, "The Time It Takes To Win It All." Winning a Super Bowl requires a lot of man hours. The writer discussed exactly how many hours it takes to get a first down in the NFL (not a touchdown, but a first down). According to an operational study conducted by the Boston Consulting Group for the article, the typical NFL season requires 514,000 hours of labor per team. That's about eight times the effort it took to conceptualize, build, and market Apple's iPad, and enough time to build 25 America's Cup yachts.[18]

If you divide a team's total preparation time by the number of yards its offense gains on the field in a season, you will find that an NFL team moves at the rate of about 32 hours per foot. That's the mind-blowing part. Let's do our own math. There are three feet in a yard, and 10 yards in a first down, or 30 feet. If an NFL team needs 32 hours per foot, that is about 100 hours per yard. That means it takes 1,000 hours for an NFL team to gain one first down!

When it's all said and done, they hoist the trophy in the middle of the field, get a check, and a ring.

The apostle Paul puts it all in perspective:

"You've all been to the stadium and seen the athletes race. Everyone runs; one wins. Run to win. All good athletes train hard. They do it for a gold medal that tarnishes and fades. You're after one that's gold eternally. I don't know about you, but I'm running hard for the finish line. I'm giving it everything I've got. No sloppy living for me! I'm staying alert and in top condition. I'm not going to get caught napping, telling everyone else all about it and then missing out myself" (1 Corinthians 9:24–27, MSG).

Paul is saying he wants you to win at being a Christian. But to win, you must give it everything you've got. It's a challenge for all of us. And the best way to win is by accepting Jesus' greatest challenge in John 15. During Jesus' life on earth, He constantly said to those who were ready to start a journey with God: "Follow Me." To those who accepted the challenge, He gave them a revolutionary second challenge: "Abide in Me."

Here are His words:

> "Abide in Me, and I in you. As the branch cannot bear fruit of itself unless it abides in the vine, so neither can you unless you abide in Me. I am the vine, you are the branches; he who abides in Me and I in him, he bears much fruit, for apart from Me you can do nothing" (John 15:4–5, NASB).

When Jesus says, "Abide in Me," He is asking for time. When you became a Christian, you came to Jesus. Now that you are with Jesus, He is asking for your most precious resource: time. God wants time with you.

If you give Him time, you won't regret it. Let's see what Jesus promises in return. In John 15, abiding is connected to four amazing benefits. You will receive joy (v. 11). You will have power to obey (v. 10). You will see answered prayer (v. 7). You will live a productive life (v. 4).

Here is the bad news: Time flies. But here is the good news: You're the pilot. Direct your life correctly, and it will be time well spent. Pablo Casals was considered the greatest cellist to ever live. At 95 years old, he was asked why he continued to practice six hours a day.

He answered, "Because I think I'm making progress."[19]

Dear Lord, I accept Your challenge to abide in You. With Your help, I am going to give it everything I've got. There are many things vying for my time, but I want joy today. I want to obey today. I need prayers answered today. I want to be productive today. That is why I choose to abide today.

MY PRAYER TODAY

18 "The Time It Takes To Win It All." (2010, February 5). The Wall Street Journal. Retrieved from https://www.wsj.com/articles/SB10001424052748704041504575045342282499792

19 Maxwell, J. C. (2002). Your Road Map for Success: You Can Get There from Here. HarperCollins Leadership

THE BEST WAY
TO FACE AN
UNCERTAIN FUTURE

Most of us cannot comprehend how many unbelievable things happen in just 24 short hours:

- Each day, 365,000 new human beings arrive on our planet.
- Around 18 million people will celebrate their birthday.
- There will be 8.6 million lightning strikes.
- 142,000 new cars will roll off the conveyor belt.
- The world's inhabitants will flush the toilet 22 billion times.
- 40,000 trees will be cut down to make paper bags, and another 27,000 will be felled to make toilet paper.
- On average, each one of us will laugh 15 times.
- Your heart will beat 104,000 times.
- 93,000 rats will be born in London alone.
- 150-200 different kinds of plants, insects, birds and mammals will become extinct because of ecological damage.
- Each of us will take, on average, 8,000 steps.
- There will be 7 separate earthquakes and 18,000 storms around the world.
- Your hair will grow 0.35 millimeters. At the same time, you will lose between 40 and 100 hairs.
- Each of us will say about 48,000 words.
- A mayfly will live out its entire life.[20]

And while all of this is happening around us, we are always planning our own lives. We are planning to go to college, planning to get married, planning to buy a home, planning to start a family. We are planning our budget, planning to work out, planning to retire. Yet in the midst of all our planning, life can take an unexpected turn.

Because all of us expect tomorrow to happen, we need to make sure we go into it with the right perspective. The Bible gives us important instructions for living in this ever-changing world:

> "Come now, you who say, 'Today or tomorrow we will go to such and such a city, and spend a year there and engage in business and make a profit.' Yet you do not know what your life will be like tomorrow. You are just a vapor that appears for a little while and then vanishes away. Instead, you ought to say, 'If the Lord wills, we will live and also do this or that'" (James 4:13–15, NASB).

James was telling us to count on this: Life is just one big if. In fact, have you ever noticed that right in the middle of the word life are the letters if? Life is full of uncertainties.

Even Solomon, the wisest man who ever lived, said in Proverbs 27:1 (NKJV), "Do not boast about tomorrow, for you do not know what a day may bring forth."

Both James and Solomon were warning us not to boast about the future without regards to the complexities and uncertainties of life.

The Bible is not condemning good planning. What the Bible is condemning is planning as though God has nothing to say about the plans you make. You say, "We will ... " when it actually is "We might ... " Beware of being certain about things for which the Bible says you can have no certainty. That's why James' first two words are somewhat humorous. He starts by saying, "Come now," which would mean "Are you serious?" or "Get real." Don't be so certain about uncertainty.

So, what is the best way to face an uncertain tomorrow? James tells us to add something when we announce our plans. We are told it's best to say, "If the Lord wills ... " or "Lord willing ... ." These are not just ritualistic statements on a believer's lips; they are the constant attitude of our hearts. We should all get comfortable saying, "If the Lord wills ... ," not as an attachment but as a reminder to us that we don't know what our lives will be like tomorrow.

When you say, "If the Lord wills … ," it means you just included God. I don't know about you, but I need God today and tomorrow, especially.

Someone said it like this: "I don't know what tomorrow holds, but I do know Who holds tomorrow."

MY PRAYER TODAY

Lord, I want You to be included in everything I do. The world is changing every day; my world is changing every day. I can't face tomorrow unless I know that You are going with me. "Lord willing … " will not just be words to me but will be the posture of my heart. While everything is changing, I have one strong confidence: You say in Your Word, "For I am the Lord, I change not" (Malachi 3:6, KJV).

20 "24 Hours: What Happens on Earth in One Day." (2024). Turkenportal. Retrieved April 13, 2024, from https://turkmenportal.com/en/compositions/1653

READING THE DIARY OF A VERY RICH MAN

There once lived a man who had the time and the money to do whatever he pleased to find happiness. The combined fortunes of Jeff Bezos, Warren Buffett, Mark Zuckerberg, and Bill Gates don't even come close to this man's wealth. He was free to do whatever he desired with no accountability. No one could question him; nobody would audit him. He held the highest office in the land—he was the king. He had no board to report to, no congress to investigate his actions, and no IRS to report income to. And he had his way for 40 years. The man's name was Solomon, and his diary was called Ecclesiastes.

This portion of his diary in chapter two is insightful for all of us:

> "I said to myself, 'Let's go for it—experiment with pleasure, have a good time!' But there was nothing to it, nothing but smoke.
>
> "What do I think of the fun-filled life? Insane! Inane!
>
> My verdict on the pursuit of happiness? Who needs it?
>
> With the help of a bottle of wine
>
> and all the wisdom I could muster,
>
> I tried my level best
>
> to penetrate the absurdity of life.
>
> I wanted to get a handle on anything useful we mortals might do
>
> during the years we spend on this earth.
>
> Oh, I did great things:
>
> built houses,
>
> planted vineyards,

designed gardens and parks

and planted a variety of fruit trees in them,

made pools of water

to irrigate the groves of trees.

I bought slaves, male and female,

who had children, giving me even more slaves;

then I acquired large herds and flocks,

larger than any before me in Jerusalem.

I piled up silver and gold,

loot from kings and kingdoms.

I gathered a chorus of singers to entertain me with song,

and—most exquisite of all pleasures—

voluptuous maidens for my bed.

"Oh, how I prospered! I left all my predecessors in Jerusalem far behind, left them behind in the dust. What's more, I kept a clear head through it all. Everything I wanted I took—I never said no to myself. I gave in to every impulse, held back nothing. I sucked the marrow of pleasure out of every task—my reward to myself for a hard day's work!

"Then I took a good look at everything I'd done, looked at all the sweat and hard work. But when I looked, I saw nothing but smoke. Smoke and spitting into the wind. There was nothing to any of it. Nothing" (Ecclesiastes 2:1–11, MSG).

When all was said and done, Solomon realized something we should all take to heart now.

An unknown author put it this way:

"Money can buy a house but not a home. Money can buy a bed but not a good night's sleep. Money can buy a book but not wisdom. Money can buy a clock but not time. Money can buy medicine but not health. Money can buy position but not respect. Money can buy blood but not life. Money can buy sex but not love."

Solomon was telling us to measure wealth not by our possessions, but by the things in our lives that we would never exchange for all the money in the world.

Solomon ends this insightful chapter with an important thought about God: "There is nothing better for people to do than to eat, drink, and find satisfaction in their work. I saw that even this comes from the hand of God. Who can eat or enjoy themselves without God?" (Ecclesiastes 2:24–25, GW).

The story is told about an old farm couple who was driving along in their pickup when the wife said, "We never sit all snuggled up in the truck like we used to."

The husband looked at her and said, "I haven't moved."

Solomon started out his life snuggled up to God, but little by little, he strayed further away. By the end, he wondered why he wasn't enjoying life. If you are feeling empty, move over and get back to God.

Dear Lord, help me each day to move closer to You, not drift further from You. It would be wise for me to realize that there were people who had what I am pursuing, yet none of it was ever fulfilling without You. May You always be my priority. Help me not to allow anything to come between us. May my heart's affections always be for You.

MY PRAYER TODAY

14

YOU HAVE TO JUMP TODAY!

There is a symbol on the back of certain GM cars that I would see all the time when I lived in Detroit, but I never actually knew what it was. I later learned it was an impala. The African impala is a unique animal that can jump to a height of more than 10 feet and cover a distance greater than 30 feet.[21] Yet these magnificent creatures can be kept in an enclosure in any zoo with a 3-foot wall. The animals will not jump if they cannot see where their feet will fall. Faith is the ability to trust what we cannot see and make the jump.

Dr. Martin Luther King, Jr. said it this way, "Faith is taking the first step even when you don't see the whole staircase."[22]

There is a book in the Bible that reads like an impala behind a 3-foot wall. It's the scariest book of the Bible— the book of Numbers.

Why is Numbers the scariest book in the Bible? It has 36 chapters that spans 40 years, yet when it reaches the last chapter, the children of Israel are still in the same geographical place they were in when the book opened. There was no movement! It is hard to imagine. Forty years went by and they hadn't gone anywhere.

There is a story about one man in the book of Numbers who is the poster child for "missing an opportunity to jump and getting stuck." His name is Hobab.

Moses had just led the children of Israel out of Egypt and was about to take them on the journey to the Promised Land. He asks his brother-in-law, Hobab, to come with them and be eyes for them in the desert. Here is their conversation and the invitation to take a leap over the wall without knowing what the future will be:

"Moses said to his brother-in-law, Hobab, son of Reuel the Midianite, Moses' father-in-law, 'We're marching to the place about which God promised, "I'll give it to you." Come with us; we'll treat you well. God has promised good things for Israel.'

"But Hobab said, 'I'm not coming; I'm going back home to my own country, to my own family.'

"Moses countered, 'Don't leave us. You know all the best places to camp in the wilderness. We need your eyes. If you come with us, we'll make sure that you share in all the good things God will do for us.'

"And so off they marched" (Numbers 10:29–33, MSG).

C. S. Lewis said, "If you want a religion to make you feel really comfortable, I certainly don't recommend Christianity."[23]

God doesn't want you to be stuck in your Christian walk, so there are times when He will make you really uncomfortable and ask you to take a leap of faith.

Here is the big question: When it says "they marched," did that include Hobab? Did Hobab jump? This is one of those passages in Scripture that we don't know the answer to, but we can speculate. His name is never mentioned again in the Bible. It seems Hobab wouldn't take the leap, so he missed the miracles. Miracles are usually on the other side of the jump.

Someone once said, "Don't ask God to guide your steps if you're not willing to move your feet."

Hobab was the impala locked up in his comfortable way of life. Throughout your spiritual journey, God will ask you to jump the 3-foot wall so you can see amazing things on the other side. Where is God asking you to jump into today? Giving? Praying? Reading the Bible? Telling someone about Jesus? My advice is: Get out of the zoo and into the wild. Make the jump.

MY PRAYER TODAY

Lord, if You ask me to jump today, I will. I may not know what's on the other side, but as long as I know You are there, that is enough for me. Don't let me get stuck in my Christian walk. Don't let me put it in park when my life should be in fifth gear. I know miracles are on the other side of the walls that confine me. I am ready for my miracle. I'm ready to make the jump.

21 Impala | African Antelope, Adaptable Mammal. (2024). Encyclopedia Britannica. Retrieved March 18, 2024, https://www.britannica.com/animal/impala

22 Martin Luter King Jr. Quote. Goodreads. Retrieved from https://www.goodreads.com/quotes/16312-faith-is-taking-the-first-step-even-when-you-can-t

23 C.S. Lewis Quote. Goodreads. Retrieved from https://www.goodreads.com/author/quotes/1069006.C_S_Lewis?page=2

LIVING
THE GOOD
LIFE

Someone once said, "Only God can turn a mess into a message. Only God can turn a test into a testimony. Only God can turn a trial into a triumph. And only God can turn a victim into a victory."

There is one verse that tells you how God does it. Put your seat belts on, this verse will change your life.

There is a promise in the Bible that will meet every situation of life you will ever face. It's this Bible promise that can help you face job loss, a bad doctor's report, reoccurring injury or sickness, financial ruin, death of a child, divorce, singleness, and COVID. Name any situation, and God has given us a promise to match it.

Here it is: "And we know that all things work together for good to them that love God, to them who are the called according to His purpose" (Romans 8:28, KJV).

Given enough time, this promise rectifies and resolves any problem you are facing with the words, "All things work together for good." That means you can't have anything but the good life if you are a Christian.

You may not know the name Fanny Crosby, but I bet you know her songs if you grew up in the church. She wrote "Blessed Assurance," "Draw Me Nearer," and "Pass Me Not O Gentle Savior," along with almost 9,000 other hymns. However, many don't know her story. Fanny was blind. She was blinded at six weeks old through the malpractice of a doctor.

When she was young, Fanny developed a phenomenal memory, learning much of the Bible by heart. Out of this treasury came a torrent of hymns and gospel songs unequaled in Christian history.

Regarding her tragedy and song writing, Fanny explained:

"The poor doctor who had spoiled my eyes soon disappeared from the neighborhood, and we never heard any more about him. I have heard that this physician never ceased expressing his regret at the occurrence; and that it was one of the sorrows of his life. But if I could meet him now, I would say, 'Thank you, thank you'—over and over again—for making me blind, if it was through your agency that it [all this music] came about!"[24]

Fanny's tragedy gave us 9,000 songs to sing. All things really do work together for good. It did for Fanny, and it can for you.

The apostle Paul was careful not to jump to "God works all things together for good" without first saying "And we know."

Those three words are basically affirming the old adage, "I don't know what tomorrow holds, but I do know Who holds tomorrow."

Romans 8:28 simply means that God's plan for you is bigger than your problems. In other words, nothing can happen to you that God cannot integrate into His good plan and purposes for your life. Romans 8:28 very well may be the greatest promise of the Bible. God can turn every tear and tragedy into triumph in the end. The Christian has a bright side to everything.

Every Christian's story truly does end with: " ... happily ever after."

MY PRAYER TODAY

Lord, a promise is only as a good as the promiser. I know that You keep Your word, so I know that this promise is as good as it gets. Each day, I will put Romans 8:28 on top of every disappointment, every loss, and every problem. Because I am Your child, I can live the good life.

---

24 Morgan, R. J. (2010). The Promise: God Works All Things Together for Your Good. B&H Publishing Group

MULTIPLICATION
IS HARDER
THAN ADDITION

I once ate beets and thought I was dying. Beets are good for you, but an abundance of crazy thoughts are not. The next day messed with my mind. After going to the bathroom, I noticed the toilet bowl was completely red. Thinking blood was pouring out of me, I immediately concluded I was dying from cancer. I went from enjoying a great dinner to thinking about my fatherless children and widowed wife. My doctor finally set the record straight when he inquired about my menu the night before. Apparently, beets contain a red pigment that shows up the next day in bowel movements. How did all that insanity happen in 24 hours?

An email comes from your coach, your supervisor, or your boss, saying, "I want to see you tomorrow." What happens to your mind, soul, and body? Your stomach is in knots and your body starts to sweat. Your soul becomes anxious. Thoughts multiply in your mind like rabbits as you come up with a narrative of the worst-case scenario.

Christian writer A. W. Tozer said it like this: "10,000 thoughts a day pass through our minds trying to predict what we will become." [25]

Let's be honest, most of the 10,000 are not good thoughts. How do we take charge over the bad portion of the 10,000 that try to predict our future?

There is good news in the book of Psalms. David tells us the problem and then the solution. He says in Psalm 94:19 (NASB), "When my anxious thoughts multiply within me, your consolations delight my soul."

Multiplication is always harder than addition—both naturally and spiritually. Teaching my children addition started with the simplicity of using fingers to add. Multiplication is a whole other beast. Things get bigger faster, which holds true for the mind as well. One email can easily turn into 10,000 thoughts, as can the doctor saying, "Let's talk about your results," or your wife telling you, "We need to talk about our marriage." Multiplication of thoughts means they start jumping at an astronomical rate. One sentence turns into a story, a novel, a production, or even a horror show.

So how do you win against devilish multiplication? David's answer to us is God's consolations. That word consolation does not sound good to us. It sounds second rate or second place.

We hear at banquets, "Here is your consolation prize (because you did not win the big prize)."

Yet according to David, God's consolations are the big prize. What does consolation mean? The word actually means, to breathe deeply. God gives you a second wind. He helps you catch your breath.

Eugene Peterson paraphrases this passage with these words, "Whenever my busy thoughts were out of control, the soothing comfort of Your presence calmed me down and overwhelmed me with delight" (Psalms 94:14, TPT).

God will calm us down with His Bible, His people, and His Holy Spirit. In your anxious moment, God will give you a Scripture. He will send an encouraging word through one of His servants. And His Holy Spirit will fight on your behalf. Just ask Him.

I heard someone say it like this: "If you're going to worry, there's no need to pray. And if you're going to pray, there's no need to worry."

Every night before I go to bed, I turn all of my problems over to God because I realize He is going to be awake all night anyway—and those issues are better in His hands than stuck in my mind.

Lord, I need Your help today with those 10,000 thoughts. You decide my future; not one of those thoughts does. You said in Isaiah 26:3 (KJV) that You will "keep him in perfect peace whose mind is stayed on Thee." I will keep my mind on You today and allow Your peace to take over. Today I choose to believe what You say about me. Let those thoughts lodge in my mind and soul.

25 MacGregor, C. (1994). The Christian Life for the Kindred in Spirit. Vision House

17

WE ARE
BETTER
TOGETHER

There are two track and field events at the Olympics that are of equal distance but are run very differently. One is run individually, and the other is run with a team of four. The 4x400 relay includes a baton and four fresh runners who each run around the track once. The world record for the relay is 2:54. The 1600-meter race is completed by one person who runs around the track four times, and the world record is 3:43. That's almost one minute longer in a sport where tenths of a second matter. You can do the mile alone, but it takes longer. It also takes a bigger toll on you.

Fresh legs go faster. There is an old Zimbabwean proverb that says, "If you want to go fast, go alone, and if you want to go further, go together." That's why Satan wants to disrupt unity and cause disagreements in the church. Nothing hurts the longevity of a church or the Kingdom more than when the relay is turned into a solo event. Relationships are so important.

Eugene Peterson said, "No Christian is an only child."[26]

That means when there is fighting amongst Christians, we are losing our spiritual siblings and making ourselves into an only child. Division is devastating to effectiveness.

Many members of the church can accomplish collectively what the same members cannot do individually. An airplane is a machine completely comprised of non-flying parts. The seats do not fly. An engine cannot fly. But when you assemble it, and all the parts are working together, they can lift 175,000 pounds off the ground, and take you around the world. In the same way, when the body of Christ is walking, running, and flying together, there is power to do the unimaginable!

In the book of Philippians, the apostle Paul spoke of two women who were flying together when a disagreement sent them back to the hangar for maintenance:

> "Now I appeal to Euodia and Syntyche. Please, because you belong to the Lord, settle your disagreement. And I ask you, my true partner, to help these two women, for they worked hard with me in telling others the Good News" (Philippians 4:2–3, NLT).

The very women who were preaching to others how to make things right with God could not seem to make it right with each other. Paul was concerned that the relay had become a solo event. These women were plane parts sitting on the ground with the potential to fly. Paul needed to get the plane back in the air by seeing a resolution take place.

If you are running alone because of a fight with someone who has helped you fly before, make it right immediately. Decide today that you are going to make a call or send a text to apologize for the disagreement. Tell them these words, "I realize that we are better together. Please forgive me for not valuing our relationship enough to get it back on course quicker." Those kinds of words put you back on the runway. Those kinds of calls put four people on the starting block rather than one. You cannot have a relationship without any fights, but you can make your relationship worth the fight. It's time to get back up in the air and out of maintenance.

Lord, I thank You for the people You have put in my life. I know that disagreements and fights are inevitable. Help me not to move on so fast but to stop and make sure I am not losing one of my relay partners along the way. It's always easier to cut something off than to put in the work to get it right, so I ask for Your help to fight for forgiveness. I want to go further and faster, together, with those You have placed in my life.

26 Peterson, E. H. (2019). A Long Obedience in the Same Direction: Discipleship in an Instant Society. InterVarsity Press

HOW CAN I BRING JOY TO GOD'S HEART TODAY?

I live in New York City, and this story made me laugh and saddened me at the same time.

In the July 15, 1993 Boardroom Reports, Peter LeVine writes:

> "When the Port Authority of New York and New Jersey ran a help-wanted ad for electricians with expertise at using Sontag connectors, it got 170 responses—even though there is no such thing as a Sontag connector. The Authority ran the ad to find out how many applicants falsify resumes."[27]

The NY and NJ Port Authority weren't just looking for electricians but honest electricians. Telling the truth matters.

The word integrity comes from the word integer. An integer is a whole number. There are no fractions to it. I believe that is significant. Integrity means that your whole life is honest. It's not fractioned off by honesty in the home but not in business, honesty in your application but not your IRS reportings. Integrity is consistent honesty in all areas added up over a period of time. It takes a long time to build up integrity, but it only takes a short time to lose it. Integrity is not high on the list of many people's priorities today because it takes work. A new study from Michigan State University found that the average number of lies told a day by a person is 1.6, or to put it another way, more than 500 lies a year.[28]

Why do we tell lies? Oftentimes, it is an attempt to avoid negative consequences. We want to get a quick reward without the work. We are looking for shortcuts. Whether you call them white lies or fibs, it's still an indictment. Lying is cowardice; telling the truth takes courage. Jesus tells us that honesty in small things is a test for us.

He said in Luke 16:10–12 (MSG),

> "If you're honest in small things, you'll be honest in big things; if you're a crook in small things, you'll be a crook in big things. If you're not honest in small jobs, who will put you in charge of the store?"

Passing the honesty test is important to God.

How can you bring joy to God's heart today? Speak the truth. Solomon tells us that when we tell the truth, it makes God happy.

Proverbs 12:22 (NLT) says, "The Lord hates lying lips, but those who speak the truth are His joy."

Do you want to make God happy? Tell the truth to your children. Tell the truth to your spouse. Tell the truth to your coach and supervisor. Tell the truth on your resume instead of claiming to know what a Sontag connector is. You may not get the job, but you will get a smile from heaven—and that's worth way more than what could ever be gained without integrity.

MY PRAYER TODAY

Lord, I am going to have a lot of opportunities today to tell the truth. Give me the courage to speak the truth, no matter how big or small the issue may seem. I want to be someone who is known for integrity. I want to make You smile today.

27 Rowell, E. K. (2008). 1001 Quotes, Illustrations, and Humorous Stories for Preachers, Teachers, and Writers. Baker Books

28 Serota, K. B., Levine, T. R., Boster, F. J. & Department of Communication, Michigan State University. (2010). "The Prevalence of Lying in America: Three Studies of Self-Reported Lies." Human Communication Research, 2–25. Retrieved from https://doi.org/10.1111/j.1468-2958.2009.01366

HOW TO
MAKE GOOD
DECISIONS

Every day you have a lot of decisions to make. Columbia research has found that the average person makes about 70 decisions every day.[29] That's 25,500 decisions each year. Over 70 years, that's 1,788,500 decisions.

Stephen Covey was right when he said, "I am not a product of my circumstances. I am a product of my decisions."[30]

Someone sent me an article called "The Biggest Millennial Struggle? Decision Fatigue." Tess Brigham, a licensed psychotherapist, specializes in treating millennials.

Brigham says, "Ninety percent of my patients are between the ages of 23 and 38. This is what they are stressing over: 'I have too many choices and I can't decide what to do. What if I make the wrong choice?'"[31]

Whether you are millennial or a card-carrying AARP member, we all want to make the right decisions. I want to give you a strategy from the apostle Paul to take with you each day when you are faced with one of those 70 decisions.

Colossians 3:15 (GNT) says, "The peace that Christ gives is to guide you in the decisions you make; for it is to this peace that God has called you together in the one body. And be thankful."

Paul is telling us something incredible. He is telling us that peace is a tool to guide our next steps when we don't have all the information, or if we a being blurred by emotions and persuasive voices.

Let me ask you a question that can apply to any sport: What would happen if you removed all of the umpires and referees? In Major

League Baseball's 30 stadiums, the greatest players in the world will need four men dressed in black sport coats to keep order. Football requires seven men dressed in striped shirts. The Olympics will also need them, as will the NBA and WNBA. No matter how good the players are, no matter how fast the athletes can run or how far they can hit the ball, umpires and referees are imperative to the game. What happens without them? One word that comes to mind is chaos!

Umpires must not be impaired by emotions, peer pressure, or even popular opinion. They must be moved by justice. Thankfully, God has given us a reliable umpire, though He often goes unacknowledged. When emotions are high and you need to make the right call on a path of life, God has equipped you with the peace of Christ as your umpire. That means we always have help available to make right decisions, even when things get emotional and outside voices are strong.

When Paul says, "Let the peace of God rule in your hearts," (Colossians 3:15, NKJV) the word rule actually means referee or umpire. The peace of Christ makes the right call when everyone is yelling in your ear to rule in their favor. Where God is not leading, there is no peace; instead, there is inner turmoil.

Have you ever said this about a decision: "I feel funny about this" or "Something doesn't feel right about taking this job?" That's the umpire. The unsettled feeling is God's help for you.

The peace of Christ is simply knowing that Christ is with me as I move forward in this direction. His peace is His smile and approval. His peace is His presence. Peace is God's support internally, even though things are chaotic externally.

A great prayer to pray is what Paul gives us later in 2 Thessalonians 3:16 (TPT), "Now, may the Lord himself, the Lord of peace, pour into you His peace in every circumstance and in every possible way. The Lord's tangible presence be with you all."

Lord, thank You for the peace of Christ. Help me to be sensitive to that peace. I will have to make quick decisions today. I may even have to make a life-altering decision today. I thank You that I am not left to decide on my own. I will ask for Your peace, and if I don't feel it, then I will pause.

MY PRAYER TODAY

29 "7 Research-backed Strategies to Stop Wasting Time Making Decisions." (2022, November 18). Columbia Business School. Retrieved from https://business.columbia.edu/faculty/press/7-research-backed-strategies-stop-wasting-time-making-decisions

30 Stephen R. Covey Quote. Goodreads. Retrieved from https://www.goodreads.com/quotes/104483-i-am-not-a-product-of-my-circumstances-i-am

31 Brigham, T. (2019, July 3). "I've Been a 'millennial Therapist' for More Than 5 Years—and This Is Their No. 1 Complaint." CNBC, Retrieved from https://www.cnbc.com/2019/07/02/a-millennial-therapist-brings-up-the-biggest-complaint-they-bring-up-in-therapy.html

A PRAYER
THAT DISTURBS
THE PRESENT

The average person will spend 2 hours and 22 minutes each day on social media. That is 864 hours each year. That translates to 14% of your waking hours on Facebook, Instagram, YouTube, and TikTok.

In an article on Quartz, author Charles Chu claims, "In the time you spend on social media each year, you could read 400 books. If you add TV to it, the math turns out to be 1,000 books a year."[32]

There is a prayer in the book of Psalms that helps us to make the most of our time when we read extraordinary statistics like this.

Catherine Booth, wife of the founder of the Salvation Army, said these powerful words, "There is no improving the future unless you disturb the present."[33]

Let's disturb our present, for our future is crucial.

The prayer of David in Psalm 90:12 (TLB) says, "Teach us to number our days and recognize how few they are; help us to spend them as we should."

David's 3,000-year-old prayer disturbs my present. I realize that we are all headed to the same place at a different pace. That place is eternity. With the time God has given me, I want to make my life count.

Some years ago, a friend of mine said, "I want to so live that God doesn't have to give me one minute's notice to step out of time into eternity."

Let's look at it this way. Counting forward is so much more exciting than counting backward. To count forward speaks of an exciting future. To count backwards speaks to a painful end. "In two years, I will graduate college." "In nine months, we will have a baby." "There are 30 days until Christmas." But counting backwards signals that the end is near. "Vacation is over in 24 hours." "We have to leave the beach in two hours." "You have only 12 months to live."

The prayer of Psalm 90 calls each of us to count backwards, regardless of how old you are. The psalmist asks God for the hard task of seeing how brief life is and how few our days are.

When I read David's prayer and started to number my days, I reflected on two things. First, life is fast.

James 4:14 (GNT) says, "You don't even know what your life tomorrow will be! You are like a puff of smoke, which appears for a moment and then disappears."

I realized I was old when I walked into a donut shop, and the cashier said to me, "You look like a famous actor."

I asked who, as my mind quickly came up with a number of great-looking possibilities. But not one of them came out of the cashier's mouth.

"Tommy Lee Jones," she said.

Tommy Lee Jones! At the time, he was in his mid-70s, while I was in my 50s. It was confirmed. Life is fast, and I am getting old.

The second point that I reflected on is that life can be wasted.

It says in 2 Samuel 14:14 "For we will surely die and are like water spilled on the ground which cannot be gathered up again."

What an image of wasting life. How many wish they can get back that year, that one decision, that night, or that decade? The hard truth is you can't. But you can decide today: No more life spilled on the ground; it's too precious. The past can't be recovered and relived, but the future can be rewritten and rewarded.

Some years ago, I was speaking at a university's Christian Medical Students Society's bible study.

One doctor-to-be offered, "Let me show you the bodies that are donated to science in the basement of our medical building!"

I have to admit, I was a little nervous to embark on that adventure. However, my curiosity got the best of me. What put Psalm 90:12 in perspective for me is when he showed me the heart of one of the cadavers and pointed out what looked like a yellow thread running through it.

He explained, "That thread is the number one killer in the country. When that yellow thread gets clogged, you have a heart attack and die."

Life is that fragile. Some of us live like that thread is as big as a train tunnel. That's why the prayer of Psalm 90 is so important. That little trip to the basement of the medical building disturbed my present and made me start counting backwards.

Remember the movie Braveheart? William Wallace would end up dying a horrible death, but his words summed up Psalm 90 well, "Every man dies, but not every man really lives."

MY PRAYER TODAY

Lord, teach me to number my days that I may live a life pleasing to You. Show me what is wasteful, and show me what is profitable. Life is too fast to waste it. Help me to make each day count.

32 Chu, C. (2022, July 20). "In The Time You Spend on Social Media Each Year, You Could Read 200 Books." Quartz. Retrieved from https://qz.com/895101/in-the-time-you-spend-on-social-media-each-year-you-could-read-200-books

33 Booth, C. M. (1990). For God Alone. Emerald House Group

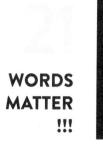

WORDS
MATTER
!!!

Be careful with your words today because words matter.

When young Tom returned home from school one day, his mother noticed he had a piece of paper in his hand. He told her it was a note from his teacher, and his mother was the only one who was supposed to read it. When she did, she grew tearful.

The boy asked what it said, and his mom replied, "Your son is a genius. This school is too small for him and doesn't have enough good teachers to train him. Please teach him yourself."

From then on, Thomas Edison's mom removed him from school and he was self-taught. Years later, after his mom died, Edison was rummaging through her belongings and came across that note from his teacher. When he read it, he was stunned by what it actually said.

It read: "Your son is addled (mentally ill). We won't let him come to school anymore. We don't have the teachers to handle him. You'll have to teach him yourself."

Edison wept for hours, and since that time, gave his mother credit for cultivating his genius as an inventor.[34] His mother saw something others didn't. Thomas Edison's mom spoke life and gave us the greatest inventor in history. Thank you, Nancy Edison, for it was because of your words that we got the light bulb, the phonograph, the camera, the telegraph, generators, microphones, alkaline batteries, cement, and a host of other things!

According to researchers, an average person speaks 16,000 words per day.[35] Those 16,000 words would translate to approximately 32 printed pages. That means in one year, an average person would fill almost 20 books of 600 pages each. That's a lot of words!

Why do those 16,000 words each day matter? Proverbs 18:21 tells us vividly why words matter.

Solomon says, "Death and life are in the power of the tongue." (Proverbs 18:21, KJV)

That's why we must take our 16,000 very seriously. I sometimes wonder what my "life and death" ratio is with my 16,000. Have I spoken life to the next great inventor, or did I kill dreams and wound a would-be all-star? Words matter!

People's hearts are very fragile, and words are incredibly powerful. Our words can change the course of someone's life. The words of life you speak can be game changers—whether you are a coach, boss, supervisor, or parent. When people hear "I love you," "I'm proud of you," "I was thinking about you," "Great job," "I'm praying for you," or "You are special"—they get a second wind.

Tucked away in the book of Job is a powerful reminder to us. Job's friends said to him that he was one that spoke life.

It says in Job 4:4 (MSG), "Your words have put stumbling people on their feet, and put fresh hope in people about to collapse."

I want to put people back on their feet. Let's choose to speak words of life today. We never know if the next Thomas Edison is within earshot of our words.

MY PRAYER TODAY

Lord, help me to speak life to those around me today. Let my words put fresh hope in people who are about to collapse. You have given my words the ability to make a difference, so let me make a difference in someone's life today.

34 Elmore, T. & McPeak, A. (2017). Marching off the Map: Inspire Students to Navigate a Brand-New World

35 Curcic, D. (2023, November 28). "How Many Words Does the Average Person Say a Day?" Retrieved from https://wordsrated.com/how-many-words-does-the-average-person-say-a-day/

A NEW PRAYER
TO GET WHAT
YOU WANT

Somebody has well said that there are only two kinds of people in the world; those who wake up in the morning and say, "Good morning, Lord;" and those who wake up in the morning and say, "Good Lord, it's morning." I want to be a "Good morning, Lord" person. I want you to be a "Good morning, Lord" person as well. This prayer from David in the Psalms has helped me to be that.

He says in Psalm 84:11 (ESV), "No good thing does He withhold from those who walk uprightly."

What better way to face the day than to know God has good things waiting for you?

No one alive has ever had every prayer answered. In fact, unanswered prayer is both a mystery and a frustration. Before you get angry with God, let me give you another perspective from this verse.

Our frustration is misplaced. We question the "He" in Psalm 84:11 and not the "who." God is the "He" in the verse, and you are the "who." Understanding this will help you to pray a new prayer each morning.

Did you know that God desires to give you good things today? Like many people, my goal used to be pursuing the good things, but I was not equally pursuing the "uprightly" part of this verse. I was going after the wrong thing. I later started asking myself the question: "Am I walking uprightly so God can give me the good things?" Many people wonder why they are not seeing the good things come their way each day. It's not because God does not want to give them good things. Rather, it's because they don't have the uprightness necessary to possess the good things. It simply means God cannot put things in our hands that we will lose through our faulty character.

Being upright doesn't mean you are perfect, but it does mean God is working on you. He is not just Lord on Sundays but every day. Integrity flows into marriage, career, student life, play time, driving, computer time, competition time, thought life. To be full of integrity is to be one who desires every area of his or her life to honor God.

I was recently watching a biography of Vince Lombardi, the great Green Bay Packers football coach. They said his priorities were always God, family, and football. Then the order would switch just on Sundays, and it would be football, family, and God.[36] That can't happen. Upright means God is the priority on the grid iron, on the basketball court, and on the playing field. When God is the priority every day, expect good things to come.

A person who only deals with God on Sundays but does what he or she wants the rest of the week is called a hypocrite. A person who does the Christian life every day is called upright. When something good is not happening, don't immediately blame God and say, "Why are You so slow?" Start with you and say, "God, are You trying to get at something in me?"

This new prayer comes from a young boy who really messed up his life. In Luke 15, he is called "the prodigal son." He messed up his life by starting with this request to his father: "Father give me" (v. 12). But we learn a new prayer when this boy who eventually returned home. He said, "Father, make me" (v. 19). There it is! It's your new prayer so you can get what you want. The new prayer is, "Father, make me ready for the good things You want to give to me." We are so accustomed to saying to the Father, "Give me!" But if we learn to start with "Make me," today is going to be a "Good morning, Lord" kind of day.

Good morning, Lord! Today is going to be a good day. I ask You to make me everything You want me to be. I believe that You want to give me good things. I am asking for Your help to walk uprightly. Nothing is off limits, Lord. I want You to speak to me not just on Sundays but every day!

36 Vince Lombardi documentary

23

GOING FROM THIRD TO SECOND

Going from third to second in sports can be a huge deal. It may mean more money, silver instead of bronze, a larger trophy, and even more prestige. But the third to second I am speaking about is with regards to point of view. When you go from third person to second person, you go from talking about someone you know about to talking about someone you know personally. That is what happens in the famous, "The Lord is My Shepherd" psalm, Psalm 23.

Psalm 23 has been read in hospitals, at funerals, printed on cards, put on pictures—it's the best of the best. Even nonreligious people are familiar with at least parts of it. Of course, the whole psalm is worth reading:

"The Lord is my shepherd,
I shall not be in need.
He makes me lie down in green pastures;
He leads me beside quiet waters.
He restores my soul;
He guides me in the paths of righteousness
For His name's sake.
Even though I walk through the valley of the shadow of death,
I fear no evil, for You are with me;
Your rod and Your staff, they comfort me.
You prepare a table before me in the presence of my enemies;
You have anointed my head with oil;
My cup overflows.
Certainly goodness and faithfulness will follow
me all the days of my life,

And my dwelling will be in the house of the Lord forever"
(Psalms 23:1-6, NASB).

An unknown author once elaborated on each line of this beloved psalm.

The Lord is my Shepherd—that's relationship!
I shall not be in need—that's supply!
He makes me lie down in green pastures—that's rest!
He leads me beside quiet waters—that's refreshment!
He restores my soul—that's healing!
He guides me in the paths of righteousness—that's guidance!
For His name's sake—that's purpose!

Even though I walk through the valley of the shadow of death—
    that's testing!
I will fear no evil—that's protection!
For you are with me—that's faithfulness!
Your rod and Your staff, they comfort me—that's discipline!
You prepare a table before me in the presence of my enemies—
    that's hope!
You have anointed my head with oil—that's consecration!
My cup overflows—that's abundance!
Certainly goodness and faithfulness will follow me all the days of
    my life—that's blessing!
And my dwelling will be in the house of the Lord—that's security!
Forever—that's eternity!

I have read this small little chapter more than a hundred times, but I learned something this week that blew my mind. Something happens in Psalm 23 that I need to draw your attention to. Within the psalm, David moves from the third person to the second person point of view. David moves from saying "The Lord is my shepherd" to "You prepare a table for me." That's huge. But what causes this change is insightful. When he goes from green pastures to the valley of the shadow of death, that is when it all pivots. God became personal.

Why did all this happen? David had a brush with death. He said it was a shadow. Shadow means close but not quite there. Have you had your brush with death; in a car, while swimming, a doctor's diagnosis? It is in those moments—when the shadow creeps up—that you understand you need God closer than ever. When death was close, David needed God closer. Death shows us the few things that truly are important.

One man said,

> "If you attempt to talk with a dying man about sports or business, he is no longer interested. He now sees other things as more important. People who are dying recognize what we often forget—that we are standing on the brink of another world."

A few years ago, there was a grandmother who, after being diagnosed with pancreatic cancer, tweeted something that went viral. She said, "I was born, I blinked, and it was over."[37]

She felt the shadow. I hope she felt God also.

The great Christian writer, C. S. Lewis, said this, "You never know how much you really believe anything until its truth or falsehood becomes a matter of life and death to you."[38]

Your mortality makes you think about what is beyond. All I know is I have a shepherd who will walk me through that valley, no matter when I face it. I want to know this shepherd personally. I want to go from third to second.

MY PRAYER TODAY

Lord, You are not only my shepherd, You are there for me in my toughest valleys. Help me to go from third person to second person—not just talking about You but knowing You personally. I need You not just for the valleys of life but every day of my life.

37 "'I Was Born, I Blinked and It Was Over': Woman's Moving Obit for Self." (2015, April 10). TODAY.Com. Retrieved from https://www.today.com/news/emily-debrayda-phillips-obituary-herself-goes-viral-t14166

38 Lewis, C. S. (1963). A Grief Observed.

24

YOU NEVER KNOW
HOW STRONG YOU ARE
UNTIL YOU HAVE TO BE STRONG

Everyone is a star basketball player when shooting hoops in their driveway or in a gym by themselves. But no one knows how good of a player they are until someone guards them. Everyone is a great athlete until there is some defense—a goalie, an opponent, or even a clock. Adversity reveals a lot about us. Proverbs tell us that it shows us where we are on the strength meter.

Solomon says in Proverbs 24:10 (NLT), "If you fail under pressure, your strength is too small."

This principle holds true in sports and spirituality. My spiritual strength is never determined inside a church with lights, music, the people of God, and preaching. It is determined by the other days of the week. Don't look for strong Christians on Sundays; look for them Monday through Saturday. You never know how strong you are until you have to be strong.

Think back to the last crisis you walked through. Maybe it was a crisis with your marriage, a child, at church, or in your job. Do a strength analysis. Don't think about the other people in that crisis, think about you. Assess yourself honestly, and see if you were strong in that day of distress. Challenging times allow you to see people's true character, skills, and leadership. Their depth shows up in difficulties.

I once read the story of a daughter who began to complain to her father about how hard things were for her.

"As soon as I solve one problem," she said, "another one comes up. I'm tired of struggling."

Her father, a chef, took her to the kitchen where he filled three pots with water and placed each on a high fire. Soon the pots came to a boil. In one he placed carrots, in the second, eggs, and in the last, ground coffee beans. He let them sit and boil without saying a word. After a while, he went over and turned off the burners. He fished out the carrots and placed them in a bowl. He pulled the eggs out and placed them in a bowl. He poured the coffee into a bowl.

Turning to his daughter, he asked, "Darling, what do you see?"

"Carrots, eggs, and coffee," she replied.

He brought her closer and asked her to feel the carrots. She noted that they were soft. He then asked her to take an egg and break it. After pulling off the shell, she observed the hard-boiled egg. Finally, he asked her to sip the coffee. She smiled, tasting its rich flavor.

"What does it mean, Father?"

He explained that each of them had faced the same adversity—boiling water—but each reacted differently. The carrot went in strong, hard, and unrelenting, but after being subjected to the boiling water, it softened and became weak. The egg was fragile. Its thin outer shell had protected its liquid interior, but after sitting through the boiling water, its inside hardened. The ground coffee beans were unique, however. By being in the boiling water, they changed the water.

He asked his daughter, "When adversity knocks on your door, which are you?"

Dr. Martin Luther King, Jr. summed it up well: "The ultimate measure of a man is not where he stands in moments of comfort and convenience, but where he stands at times of challenge and controversy."[39]

Lord, I may never have said this prayer before, but here it goes, "Make me a strong cup of coffee." Even in the midst of difficulties, help me to change the environment around me for the better. Give me the strength I need today to face any adversity that may come my way.

MY PRAYER TODAY

39 White House Historical Association. (n.d.). "Honoring Martin Luther King, Jr." WHHA (En-US). Retrieved from https://www.whitehousehistory.org/honoring-martin-luther-king-jr

25

JACKS
OR
MASTERS

I live in a city where you are strictly prohibited from using your cell phone while driving. They want drivers to focus and avoid distractions, which is especially important when driving in New York City.

According to the DMV, "Driving at 55 miles per hour while sending or reading a text is like driving the length of a football field with your eyes closed."[40]

When you are behind the wheel of a car, the DMV wants you to do one thing: drive. This is not only good advice when you are behind the wheel of a car but for all of life. Steve Jobs, during a conversation with the CEO of Nike, attributed his success to staying focused.

Jobs said,

> "People think focus means saying 'yes' to the thing you've got to focus on. But that's not what it means at all. It means saying 'no' to the hundred other good ideas that there are. You have to pick carefully. I'm actually as proud of the things we haven't done as the things I have done. Innovation is saying 'no' to 1,000 things."[41]

The best drivers are not talking or texting on their phones but are fully engaged with everything around them.

The apostle Paul was telling us the same thing in Philippians 3. He was laser focused on forgetting the past and reaching towards the goal that God had for him:

> "Brothers and sisters, I do not consider myself yet to have taken hold of it. But one thing I do: Forgetting what is behind and straining toward what is ahead, I press on toward the goal to

win the prize for which God has called me heavenward in Christ Jesus" (Philippians 3:13–14, NIV).

To leave the past behind and give everything for the future means living a life of "one thing." Even Solomon said in Ecclesiastes 7:18, "It is good that you grasp one thing." "One thing" people are very rare to find, but they are the people who make the biggest difference. They have chosen to be masters instead of jacks.

When Luciano Pavarotti, the famous Italian tenor, was a boy, his father introduced him to the wonders of song. He urged Luciano to work very hard to develop his voice. Taking his father's advice, Luciano became a pupil under Arrigo Pola, the professional tenor. He also enrolled in a teachers' college.

Upon graduating, he asked his father, "Shall I be a teacher or a singer?"

His father replied, "If you try to sit on two chairs, you will fall between them. For life, you must choose one chair."

Luciano chose one. After seven years of study, he made his first professional appearance. After another seven years, he reached the Metropolitan Opera.

He went on to say, "Now I think whether it's laying bricks, writing a book, whatever we choose, we should give ourselves to it. Commitment, that's the key. Choose one chair."[42]

Pavarotti called it "one chair." Solomon called it "one thing." The old adage is both true and incriminating of our society's attention span: "Jack of all trades, master of none." Masters of one make a living out of that kind of focus. Jacks may get paid occasionally. Do you get paid for your passion? Decide if you are a jack or a master. The master lives for his passion. The jack has a job.

The most important "one thing" to choose first is God. Make Him your first passion, and everything else will fall into line.

MY PRAYER TODAY

Lord, keep me focused today. First and foremost, set my eyes on You. I need Your help to be a "one thing" person. There are so many distractions and voices calling for my attention, trying to take my eyes off the road ahead. I start today by choosing You before I say "yes" to anything else.

40 "Distracted Driving." (n.d.). NHTSA. Retrieved from https://www.nhtsa.gov/risky-driving/distracted-driving

41 Mejia, Z. (2018, October 2). "Steve Jobs: Here's What Most People Get Wrong About Focus." CNBC, Retrieved from https://www.cnbc.com/2018/10/02/steve-jobs-heres-what-most-people-get-wrong-about-focus.html

42 Pavarotti, L. (2022, June 28). "Guideposts Classics: Luciano Pavarotti on Making the Most of God's Gifts." Guideposts. Retrieved from https://guideposts.org/positive-living/entertainment/music/guideposts-classics-luciano-pavarotti-on-making-the-most-of-gods/

26

MOVING FROM RELIGION TO RELATIONSHIP

The apostle Paul tells us something epic in the book of 2 Corinthians.

He reminds us, "There's far more here than meets the eye. The things we see now are here today, gone tomorrow. But the things we can't see now will last forever" (2 Corinthians 4:18, MSG).

The things we can't see now are eternal!

It is as someone once said: "Our life on Earth is the first page of a never-ending story."

The next time you hear MSNBC, a politician, or a financial periodical use the word billion, I want you to take the time to think about it more deeply. A billion is difficult for us to fully comprehend. Consider the following to help put the figure into perspective:

A billion seconds ago, it was 1993.

A billion minutes ago, Jesus was alive.

A billion hours ago, the characters in the
   book of Genesis were living.

A billion days ago, no one walked on earth, if it was here.

A billion dollars ago was only 8 hours and 20 minutes,
   at the rate the government spends it.

A billion years from now, where will you be?[43]

In a billion years, we will all be in eternity, which therefore makes it imperative that we get the right perspective on eternity. You will see on cemetery headstones a little symbol that measures our complete life on earth. It is the dash—the little symbol that goes between our birth date and date of death. My billion, or my eternity, is attached to the dash. Everything I have done in my life is summed up with that little symbol. Every decision, every impact, every hurt, every good time, every victory, every loss, and every trophy is represented by that dash—which begs the question: What are you doing with your dash?

In John 3, Jesus spoke to a religious man about eternity and his dash. The man's name was Nicodemus. I believe Jesus wanted to see religion change to relationship on this man's dash. Religion is like dating God. You see Him only on the weekends. On the other hand, relationship is walking together every day. Listen to Jesus' words that move all of us from religion to relationship. It will be these words that prepare us for eternity.

> "'I am telling you the truth,' replied Jesus, 'that no one can enter the Kingdom of God without being born of water and the Spirit. A person is born physically of human parents, but is born spiritually of the Spirit. Do not be surprised because I tell you that you must all be born again'" (John 3:5–7, GNT).

If being born again puts you in heaven, then you must be born again. Most importantly, you had better know what born again means because Jesus said, "You must be born again." You cannot make optional what Jesus says is a necessity. When you were born the first time, you received natural life. When you are born a second time, you receive spiritual life. Only someone with spiritual life can exist and survive in heaven. To enjoy, commune, and understand God, you must have the kind of life that He has. If your response to the question, "Are you born again" is: "I think," "I hope," or "I'm not sure," then please consider the following, for eternity is hanging on your answer.

What does it mean to be "born again"? It means every sin is forgiven. It means Jesus lives in me through the Holy Spirit to give me peace, power, and purpose. It means I have the confidence of knowing that I am going to heaven when I die. I want you to be a shouting Christian, not a doubting church attender. When it comes to be being a born-again Christian, we ought to be an exclamation point, not a question mark. Just as no one is born twice physically, no one needs to be "born again" twice. You were born physically once, and you are born spiritually once.

You had no choice about your first birth, but you do have a choice about your second birth. Born again is a Jesus term, not a religious term. When you are born again, you make the most important decision on your dash, and you have an assurance about where you will spend your billion—your eternity. Religion has just become a relationship.

Lord, I believe that You are the Son of God. I believe that on the cross, You took my sin, my shame, and my guilt; and You died for it. I believe that You faced hell for me so I would not have to go. I believe You rose from the dead to give me a place in heaven, a purpose on earth, and a relationship with Your Father. Today, Lord Jesus, I turn from my sin to be born again. God is my Father, Jesus is my Savior, the Holy Spirit is my helper, and heaven is now my home. In Jesus name, amen!

MY PRAYER TODAY

43 Mikkelson, D. (2003, October 9). "Billions and Billions." Snopes. https://www.snopes.com/fact-check/billions-and-billions/

27

REMEMBERING THE GREATEST 25 WORDS EVER WRITTEN

John 3:16 is the most wonderful sentence ever written. Jesus said, "For God so loved the world, that He gave His only begotten Son, that whoever believes in Him shall not perish, but have eternal life" (NASB). Those 25 words tell an amazing love story. It begins with God, who has no beginning, and concludes with life that has no end. Someone once broke down the 25 words this way:

- **God:** the greatest Lover.
- **So loved:** the greatest degree.
- **The world:** the greatest number.
- **That He gave:** the greatest act.
- **His only begotten Son:** the greatest gift.
- **That whosoever:** the greatest invitation.
- **Believeth:** the greatest simplicity.
- **In Him:** the greatest Person.
- **Should not perish:** the greatest deliverance.
- **But:** the greatest difference.
- **Have:** the greatest certainty.
- **Everlasting life:** the greatest possession.

I have a little book full of children's letters to pastors[44], which I pull out occasionally for a chuckle. Here are a few:

> Dear Pastor,
> I would like to go to heaven one day because
> my brother will not be there.
> —Stephen, age 8

Dear Pastor,
I think a lot more people would come to your
church if you moved it to Disneyland.
—Loreen, age 9

And then one of my favorites:

Dear Pastor,
I know God loves everybody, but has He ever met my sister?
—Arnold age 8

Based on John 3:16, God loves even Arnold's sister. How? There is nothing about the world that God should love. It is a sinful and a selfish world; it is a corrupt world. It is not because the world is lovable but because God is love. There is no man or woman whom God does not love. There is not a thief, convict, mass murderer, dictator, adulterer, or abuser whom God does not love. He loves losers and winners. He loves everyone equally, and for that reason, He came on the ultimate rescue mission to bring us home. It all started with a love beyond comprehension.

Most of what you hear and see of love today is not real love—not God's love. It was His love that started it all. Salvation and heaven all began with God. He initiated the whole thing because of His great love for us. God had to make the first move, for this kind of love is foreign to all of us.

A father will give everything he possesses before he would give up his own son. There is not a father today who would stand by and let men treat his son cruelly with nails and hammers, but God did. He allowed His Son to die when He could have rescued Him. That is what makes His love so wonderful, so beyond human understanding. Real love demonstrates. Real love produces action. God proved His love when He gave His one and only Son, Jesus.

I once read a story of sacrificial love that blew me away. According to the Chicago Tribune, on June 22, 1997, parachute instructor, Michael Costello, 42, jumped out of an airplane at an altitude of 12,000 feet with a novice skydiver named Gareth Griffith, age 21. The novice would soon discover just how good his instructor was, for when the novice pulled his rip cord, his parachute failed. Plummeting to the ground, they faced certain death. But then the instructor did an amazing thing. Just before hitting the ground, the instructor rolled over so that he would hit the ground first, and the novice would land on top of him. The instructor was killed instantly. The novice fractured his spine in the fall, but he was not paralyzed. One man substituted himself to die so another might live.[45]

That is what God did for all of humanity. God rolled over for us all. Talk about His descent downward—it was infinitely further than 12,000 feet. He came from heaven to earth to die for us!

Or as one man put it: "God paid the price, but you got the change."

You got to change your life, your future, and your forever.

MY PRAYER TODAY

Lord, I am amazed at Your love for me. You love me despite my shortcomings, failures, and sin. You proved that to me when You died on the cross in my place. I thank You for such a radical love for me.

44 Hall, T. (2004). The Bible Almanac for Kids: A Journey of Discovery Into the Wild, Incredible, and Mysterious Facts & Trivia of the Bible

45 Larson, C. B. (1998). Choice Contemporary Stories and Illustrations: For Preachers, Teachers, and Writers. Baker Publishing Group

28

GIVING CREDIT WHERE CREDIT IS DUE

It is said that when the famed Italian Renaissance artist, Michelangelo, was old and blind, he visited Rome. While he was there, a great piece of art was discovered and brought to him in hopes he could identify it. What a task for an old and blind man.

Then the amazing happened. Michelangelo started to run his fingers up and down each section of the stone, and after a few minutes, concluded, "This is the work of a master."

He felt it again and said, "It is Phidias."

Although Michelangelo was blind, he could feel the contours on the masterpiece and knew that it was the work of a master sculptor. He knew who to give the credit to.

Where you are today and what you have accomplished did not come easy. It was the product of hours of toil while no one was watching. You studied, worked out, watched film, got up early, and stayed up late while other people were in bed. You kept at it and created a masterpiece.

Many people will see the masterpiece of our lives—in our field of study, athletics, or coaching—but will often attribute credit to the wrong person. Because Michelangelo was a great artist, he was able to recognize the work of Phidias, another great artist. The problem arises when you have novice artists giving credit to the wrong person. A master knows another master.

He was the richest and most well-known man of his time. He was known in heaven and in hell, and even Satan wanted to try to take this man down. His name was Job. His story is in one of the oldest books of the Bible, and they are the toughest 37 chapters of pain that one person could ever face. That's why the name Job is always associated with trials and tribulations. The good news, however, is that Job wins in the end. God helps him overcome all the trials.

What is amazing is that Job says these words in Job 12:9 (NKJV), "Who among all these does not know that the hand of the Lord has done this."

Job was giving credit where credit belonged. He knew that God permitted the trials, and he also knew that God would carry him through to the end. He gave God all the credit because God deserved it. Like Michelangelo, Job felt what was happening. Even through the pain, he sensed that God's hand was creating something.

Job's words seem to reflect those of Michelangelo: "This is the work of the Master"—capital M.

Whatever we accomplish, whatever success we have in life, whatever awards and accolades we receive, let's give credit where credit is due. Look at what has happened in your life. See the contours of the victories.

Take in the moment, enjoy the satisfaction of knowing all the hard work has paid off, and then with all your heart, declare as Job did: "Who among all these does not know that the hand of the Lord has done this?"

There will be some who don't know it was the hand of the Lord, so we will tell them, giving credit to Whom credit is due.

MY PRAYER TODAY

Lord, You get all the glory and honor today for anything I have accomplished. Whether it's my college degree, my children, my career, or my success, I see Your fingerprints on it all. I will be careful to give credit to Whom credit is due. You gave me these gifts, so I will give You all the glory.

I HAVE EVERYTHING I NEED FOR TODAY

Every time I read this prayer, I chuckle. An unknown yet sincere individual prayed these words:

Dear God,

So far today I've done everything right. I haven't gossiped, I haven't lost my temper, I haven't been greedy, grumpy, nasty, selfish, or over-indulgent. I'm very thankful for that. But in a few minutes, God, I'm going to get out of bed, and from then on, I'm probably going to need a lot of help. Amen.

I have felt that way. Everything is going right until I put my feet on the floor and get out of bed. Thankfully, there is good news. There is a powerful promise in the often overlooked book of Deuteronomy in the Bible. It has given me comfort each time my feet hit the ground:

"And your strength will equal your days" (Deuteronomy 33:25, NIV).

This verse first hung in his law office and then in his bedroom at the White House. The secret of President Grover Cleveland's energy was found in the verse he lived by. He framed and hung it directly over his bed so he could see it each night upon retiring and every morning when waking up.

When asked about it, Cleveland said, "If I have any coat of arms and emblem, it is that."

He lived with the firm conviction that when his feet hit the floor in the morning, God would supply sufficient strength for that day's tasks.[46] I hope that the verse was left in the White House because, more than ever, each president needs to rely on that promise.

"Your strength will equal your days" gives all of us hope to face today's challenges. God does not give us strength to face tomorrow, but today.

That's why Jesus says in Matthew 6:34 (NASB), "So do not worry about tomorrow; for tomorrow will care for itself. Each day has enough trouble of its own."

God will give you everything you need for today's trouble. One woman who knew this well and found strength to equal her days was holocaust survivor, Corrie Ten Boom.

She said, "Worry does not empty tomorrow of its sorrow, it empties today of its strength."[47]

Worry is the enemy of strength. When you let worry seep into your soul, you poke holes into your strength reserve. Stand on the promise of Deuteronomy, confident that God will give you everything you need to face today.

I remember reading an old story about a little boy helping his father with the yard work. The father asked the boy to pick up rocks in a certain area of the yard. From the corner of his eye, the father saw his son struggling to pull up a huge rock buried in the dirt. The little boy struggled and struggled while his father simply watched.

Finally, the boy gave up and sighed, "I can't do it."

His dad asked him, "Did you use all of your strength?"

The little boy looked puzzled and replied, "Yes, sir. I used every ounce of strength I have."

The father smiled and said, "No you didn't. You didn't ask me for help."

The father walked over, and then the two of them pulled that big rock out of the dirt.

You are going to have to move some big rocks today. Don't forget to ask Your heavenly Father for help.

Lord, You always keep Your promises; that is why I know I can hold on to Your Word when You say, "Your strength will equal your days." Thank You for sufficient strength for today. I don't know exactly what I will face, but I know I will not face it alone. Thank You that I do not have to worry about tomorrow, for You will supply me with all that I need to go forward each day.

MY PRAYER TODAY

46 Morgan, R. J. (2016). The Strength You Need: The Twelve Great Strength Passages of the Bible. Thomas Nelson

47 "A Quote From Clippings From My Notebook." (n.d.). Goodreads. Retrieved from https://www.goodreads.com/quotes/35574-worry-does-not-empty-tomorrow-of-its-sorrow-it-empties

LIVING FOR THE
REAL REWARD—
THE FINAL REWARD

Very few athletes win by accident. Winning is a product of hard work and discipline. Champions don't become champions in the ring, on the field, or on the track; they are merely recognized there. A champion is made in the daily routine—not in a day, but in the daily.

I remember hearing the story of a father who took his son to his first boxing match. The observant little boy watched the challenger make the sign of the cross before the first round started.

The boy asked his father after observing the Catholic ritual, "Does that help?"

The father answered, "Yes, if he knows how to box."

That sign would not make him a good boxer if he had not put in the work every day.

What is true in the natural is also true in the spiritual. The apostle Paul tells us about the final reward, which is the real reward.

He says in 2 Corinthians 5:10 (NASB), "For we must all appear before the judgment seat of Christ, so that each one may be recompensed for his deeds in the body, according to what he has done, whether good or bad." Paul is speaking about heaven's medal ceremony. This is not judgment for your salvation but rewards for how you loved and how you lived your Christian life here on this planet. The reward has nothing to do with us as sons but our relationship to Him as servants.

The judgment seat of Christ is referred to as the Bema Seat. It is the place where Christ will judge if the rules were kept, and then He will award the prizes to the winners. Every believer will appear there. The person I am becoming today is preparing me for the person I shall be for all eternity. The way we live here will have eternal, unchangeable, and profound consequences.

The Bible commentator, Matthew Henry, wrote: "It ought to be our business every day to prepare for the last day."

Only in this life can we impact our eternity.

In the past, God dealt with us as sinners. In the present, God deals with us as sons. In the future, God deals with us as stewards and even as competitive athletes. In ancient Greece, the Bema Seat was a raised platform where assembly speeches were given and crowns awarded to winners of the Isthmian games. Our reward will not be for being the fastest or scoring the most points; it will be based on other criteria. There will not be medals but crowns bestowed. What will the rewards be?

The Incorruptible Crown: to those who master the old nature (1 Corinthians 9:25-27).

The Crown of Rejoicing: to soul winners (Daniel 12:3; 1 Thessalonians 2:19, 20).

The Crown of Life: to those who successfully endure temptation (James 1:2; Romans 2:10).

The Crown of Righteousness: to those who love the rapture (2 Timothy 4:8).

The Crown of Glory: to faithful preachers and teachers (1 Peter 5:2-4).

How we live today will determine the words we hear from Christ at the Bema Seat.

During one of his last interviews, Billy Graham was speaking with Diane Sawyer, and she asked the great evangelist: "How would you like to be remembered?"

Billy Graham responded, "I want to hear the Lord say, 'Well done, thy good and faithful servant.'"[48]

That wasn't just Billy Graham's goal and the apostle Paul's goal, it should be the goal of all of us. Remember the words of Paul that we considered in the introduction—his description of how we ought to live in this world before we stand on heaven's podium:

"You've all been to the stadium and seen the athletes race. Everyone runs; one wins. Run to win. All good athletes train hard. They do it for a gold medal that tarnishes and fades. You're after one that's gold eternally. I don't know about you, but I'm running hard for the finish line. I'm giving it everything I've got. No sloppy living for me!" (1 Corinthians 9:24-26, MSG).

Let's give it all we've got and go after that which is gold eternally.

MY PRAYER TODAY

Lord, keep my eyes on the real prize. Help me to finish well and one day hear those words, "Well done, good and faithful servant." Those words to me from the mouth of Jesus are gold—eternal gold!

48 Innes, R. (2007, December 13). "Living With the End in Mind." The Christian Post. Retrieved from https://www.christianpost.com/news/living-with-the-end-in-mind.html

LASTING THOUGHTS

...

The great Christian writer, C. S. Lewis said, "If you read history, you will find that the Christians who did most for the present world were precisely those who thought most of the next."[49]

These words are both instructive and profound, providing all of us with our marching orders for the future. As you are working out in preparation for a match, a game, or an event, always keep in mind Paul's admonition to a young man in the book of First Timothy. "Workouts in the gymnasium are useful, but a disciplined life in God is far more so, making you fit both today and forever" (1 Timothy 4:8, MSG).

Paul was echoing C. S. Lewis' words. Being fit for today—that's good. Getting fit for eternity—that's crucial. That is what eternal gold is all about. Eternal gold keeps us looking further than today.

When I'm writing, adding long sections of scripture is not something that I typically do. However, I think this passage is appropriate for every athlete, every coach, and every competitor. It is what keeps us focused on the right kind of gold. The writer of Hebrews puts our race, our struggles, and our finish line all in perspective. Let these verses be the exclamation point as you compete:

> "Do you see what this means—all these pioneers who blazed the way, all these veterans cheering us on? It means we'd better get on with it. Strip down, start running—and never quit! No extra spiritual fat, no parasitic sins. Keep your eyes on Jesus, who both began and finished this race we're in. Study how he did it. Because he never lost sight of where he was headed—that exhilarating finish in and with God—he could put up with anything along the way: cross, shame, whatever. And now he's

there, in the place of honor, right alongside God. When you find yourselves flagging in your faith, go over that story again, item by item, that long litany of hostility he plowed through. That will shoot adrenaline into your souls!" (Hebrews 12:1–3, MSG).

We pray God's richest blessing on your lives.

Win the eternal gold!

Tim Dilena

49 Lewis, C. S. (1952). Mere Christianity. Scribner

ABOUT THE AUTHOR

Tim Dilena is the senior pastor of Times Square Church in New York City. He has also served as a speaker for the MLB, WNBA, and NFL chapels, and is the author of **The 260 Journey**, **What Does God Have to Say?**, **Your Life is God's Story**, and **Prayer 101**.

Pastor Tim's main focus is to help people have a relationship with God. His messages and books offer deep, yet easy to understand insights that make us see how faith in Jesus is not only relevant but essential to everything in life.

DIVE DEEPER

Watch the messages
that inspired this book.

**Find encouragement
for every stage of your prayer journey:**
from how to start and never give up,
to experiencing breakthroughs.

Scan this QR code
or visit **tsc.nyc/becauseyouprayed**

ALSO AVAILABLE

FROM TIM DILENA

GET INSIGHT	**STAND FIRM**	**TRUST GOD**
Discover life-changing lessons from each New Testament chapter, one day at a time.	Learn God's principles to hold steady in an unstable world.	See how God led others through life's ups and downs.

Help others
find these resources.

1

**Post a picture
on your social media**
and share why you
found them meaningful.

2

Gift them to someone
who might benefit from them.

3

Go through them with a friend,
or start a Bible study group.

For more spiritual insight
to help you thrive in everyday life:

Explore
messages and books at
tsc.nyc

Follow us

@TimesSquareChurch

@PastorTimDilena

TIMES SQUARE ▣ CHURCH
1657 Broadway NY, NY 10019
tsc.nyc